BATS

BATS
•PHIL RICHARDSON•

with illustrations by
GUY TROUGHTON

Whittet Books

Title page illustration: Serotine chasing cockchafer beetle

First published 1985
Reprinted 1987, 1990, 1993, 1994
This new revised edition first published 2000
Text ©1985, 2000 by Phil Richardson
Illustrations © 1985, 2000 by Guy Troughton
Whittet Books, Hill Farm, Stonham Rd, Cotton, Stowmarket, Suffolk IP14 4RQ

Design by Richard Kelly

British Library Cataloguing in Publication Data

Richardson, Phil
    Bats.
    1. Bats—Great Britain
    I. Title
    599.4'0941   QL737.C5
    ISBN 1 873580 50 9

Typeset by Inforum Ltd, Portsmouth.
Printed in Great Britain by WBC Book Manufacturers

Contents

Preface

You may be reading this trying to make up your mind whether to buy the book or not – don't hesitate, buy it! I am sure you will gain from these pages some of the joys that I have experienced when studying bats in Britain.

Bats are often feared, but this is usually due to ignorance: no bat is ever going to cause you any harm. In this book I have attempted to paint a more attractive picture of our much maligned bats; my studies show that they are sweet and cuddly and not characters to be detested. I helped form the Northants Bat Group – a group of bat enthusiasts studying all aspects of the amazing lives of bats from their choice of living accommodation to their choice of food, from their elaborate ultrasonic calls to their peculiar ways of adjusting their body temperatures so as to hibernate. Throughout the studies our concern for their conservation has been paramount – many are threatened by the pressures we place on them in the countryside. All of this is covered here and more besides. Over the years the bat group has been involved in some remarkable incidents; some are re-lived here but others will have to await the unexpurgated edition of this book. Bat groups have now set up in most areas of Britain so it is possible for anyone to join in the study and conservation of bats in their area. By joining your local group you will be meeting others with similar interests to your own. Each group conducts special studies on a particular species of bat or special roosting area, but all groups are involved in 'roost visits' (where members of the public with roosts are visited and informed about their bats), and in conservation projects where roost sites are carefully protected and the numbers of bats using the sites monitored.

When I began work on bats little information was readily available about them. Much was hidden away in obscure journals in university libraries. This book is designed to give simple down-to-earth information about our bats and reflect the great deal of fun and interest that we can all experience by watching bats. I hope that when you have read it you, too, will become a batophile. Some of you may have already been converted; I hope you will be stimulated by the book and continue to extend your interest and convert others (e.g. by buying them a copy of this book). Bats need friends.

August 1999   *Phil Richardson*

Acknowledgments

My studies of bats evolved from a general interest in all forms of wildlife that was encouraged from an early age by my parents, to whom I am most grateful. I have gained much specific knowledge from many bat experts in all parts of the world and their work has provided a good foundation for my studies in Britain. Most of my practical knowledge has been gained as a result of the diverse and widespread activities of the Northants Bat Group which I have been involved with since its inception. Thanks are due to all past and present members of the group, especially to Ian Flinders, Harry Purdom, Pam Watson and Conor Kelleher. Marion and Deb Williamson have kindly acted as foster parents for numerous poorly bats and have helped to expand our knowledge of their needs. Sue Paice and Derek Bull generously provided much needed equipment, and Sue has given much moral support. Thanks are also due to the hundreds of owners of roost sites who gave us access to their bats, in particular the Fleckneys for allowing us to take over half of their house when their roost appears each year. A number of my students have helped in time-consuming studies on Daubenton's bats and I am grateful to them all.

During my work I have valued the advice given by many experts and in particular Drs Bob Stebbings, Pat Morris and Paul Racey. The facilities of the British Museum (Natural History) were made possible by Tony Hutson and John Hill, both of whom have been most helpful at all times.

Some of my studies have been kindly aided by funds from the Royal Society and the Mammal Society; the Royal Society for Nature Conservation has also been very co-operative.

Evolution

When dinosaurs stalked the earth, over their heads flew – or glided – creatures rather like bats. These were Pterosaurs, which had very long fingers with membranes of skin attached, acting as wings. Apart from this superficial resemblance to bats, they were very different, and were in fact reptiles, whereas bats are mammals (reptiles have an outer covering of horny scales, not hair, do not feed their young on milk, and have no internal regulator of body temperature – very different from bats, as we will see later). These early pioneers of flight went the way of the dinosaurs, becoming extinct about 65 million years ago. Soon after the dinosaurs had gone to their happy paddling pool in the sky, mammals began to diversify and expand their range. It is believed that some type of insect-eating mammal which scrambled around in

The attempts of early mammals to fly.

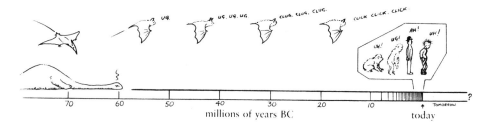

Evolution in perspective.

trees gradually evolved to become the bats that we know today. Often we can trace the evolutionary progress of a mammal by finding older and older fossils, each of which shows some stage of evolution. Unfortunately no intermediate stages in the bats' family tree have yet been identified. The very oldest bat fossil discovered so far is approximately 50 million years old and it looks very much like a modern bat and gives no hint as to the appearance of its ancestors. Since these early times fossils show that bats became more and more diverse as they adapted to different climates, habitats and foods. Some never quite made it, as the fossils of extinct families of bats show. Some have been so successful that they have been flitting about in their current form for millions of years. Fruit bats (see p.11) seem to have evolved into existence more recently and some of the latest theories suggest that they evolved from primates. Amazingly they have the same basic structure as the other bats, but are more closely related to Man! Just by a quirk of Nature some apes evolved into humans and another primate branch turned into bats! Just think of the possibilities those millions of years ago. Would you evolve into a beautiful, intelligent, caring creature, full of fun, or would you turn into a human?

More recently there have been a few major set-backs for bats. Man began to appear on the surface of the planet a mere 5 million years ago and has since taken on a rather dominant role which has affected most other creatures. Also there have been patches of rough weather in the last million years in the form of Ice Ages which affected the range, numbers and evolution of many mammals, including bats. Further climatic and environmental changes will, no doubt, continue to mould our bats. Those that do not adjust will become extinct. The basic pattern, however, remains relatively unchanged even after 50 million years.

The world of bats

There are about 900 different species of bat in the world, and an amazing variety in their appearance. There are big bats with a 6 foot (2 metre) wingspan; small bats with bodies only 1¼ inches (3 cm.) long; heavyweight bats of over 2 lb (1,000 g.); light bats of ¹/₁₅th oz (2 g.), white ones, striped ones, naked ones and even ones with gaudy fluffy head-pieces like fancy hats.

Their food is also very varied, ranging from pollen and nectar to fish, frogs, lizards and insects, for example, and each kind of food requires a special feeding method. This partly explains the peculiar features of some bats. A nectar-feeding bat will require a long tongue to dip into flowers, so it has to have a long snout to house the tongue. Fish-eating bats have very powerful feet with long, sharp claws which are used to snatch small fish from the surface of the water. Most species rely on echo-location (see p. 28) to guide them at night, so have developed specially shaped noses and ears to help them emit and receive the sounds; sometimes these make bats look very distinctive and even a little bizarre.

Most bats have at least one thing in common – they are active at night and leave daytime frog-gulping, nectar-slurping and insect-ingesting to the birds.

With such a large number of species, it is sensible to arrange them in some sort of order. Bats (*Chiroptera* is their scientific name) divide nicely into two sub-orders – the *Megachiroptera* and the *Microchiroptera*. The former are the 'Old World' fruit bats (ranging from Africa eastwards to the Pacific islands) and generally have very large eyes, which they use for navigation in place of echo-location; and have teeth designed to cut and chop up fruit. The *Microchiroptera*, the ones we have in Britain, have quite small eyes and many

Indian Fruit Bat.

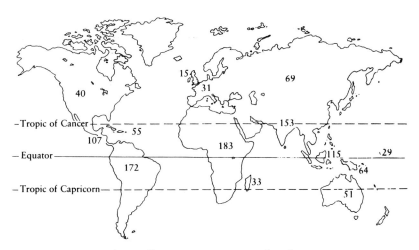

Numbers of bat species in geographical regions.
(There is overlap of species between areas).

use echo-location to navigate and to find food; they include a very large number of species worldwide with many differences so they are divided again into 17 families. The largest family contains over 300 species (one third of the total number of bat species in the world) so further division into genera arranges very similar species together. Taxonomists, whose job it is to try to arrange species in this way, do not all agree as to the exact number of species nor on some of the groupings, but at least some order is achieved for the 850–950 species.

Bats are found in all parts of the world except for the poles. They can be found in most habitats, even desert. The largest numbers of species are found close to the equator and on the larger land masses, which provide the greatest variety of food and habitats for bats. Smaller numbers of species are found outside the tropics and on islands (see map above).

Some species occur in large numbers over a large part of the world, whereas others are restricted to a few bats in a small area. Some island communities of bats are isolated and so are particularly vulnerable to natural disasters such as hurricanes and to man's interference, particularly habitat destruction. The Rodrigues Fruit Bat, for instance, was becoming very rare in its isolated Indian Ocean island habitat mainly due to the pressures of man. It has now been taken into captivity and is being successfully bred. The recently discovered Hog-nosed Bat is only found in a couple of caves in Thailand.

Fruit bat.

Tourism and collecting in the area poses a serious threat to this unique bat, the only one of its family. National and international help is being given to try to protect it in the wild. Unfortunately other species have received no help and some have not been seen for a number of years and are probably now extinct; just a few specimens in museum collections remain to remind us of them.

Bats of the world

Chiroptera ('Hand wing')

	Number of species
Megachiroptera	
Flying foxes or fruit bats (*Pteropodidae*)	c.165
Microchiroptera	
Mouse-tailed Bats (*Rhinopomatidae*)	c.3
Sheath-tailed and Ghost Bats (*Emballonuridae*)	44
Hog-nosed Bat (*Craseonycteridae*)	1
Slit-faced Bats (*Nycteridae*)	c.12
False Vampire and Yellow-winged Bats (*Megadermatidae*)	5
Horseshoe Bats (*Rhinolphidae*)	69

Old World Leaf-nosed Bats (*Hipposideridae*)	*c*.60
Bulldog or Fisherman Bats (*Noctilionidae*)	2
Moustached, Naked-backed and Ghost-faced Bats (*Mormoopidae*)	*c*.8
New World Leaf- or Spear-nosed and Vampire Bats (*Phyllostomidae*)	*c*.145
Funnel-eared Bats (*Natalidae*)	4
Smoky Bats (*Furipteridae*)	2
Disc-winged Bats (*Thyropteridae*)	2
Sucker-footed Bat (*Myzopodidae*)	1
Evening or Vesper Bats (*Vespertilionidae*)	*c*.300
Short-tailed Bats (*Mystacinidae*)	2
Free-tailed Bats (*Molossidae*)	*c*.85

Not all authors agree on the exact number of species or on the grouping of some species into families. This list summarizes some of the present ideas (after Koopman and Jones, 1970, and Hill and Smith, 1984).

The English names for families are generally descriptive: hence the Horseshoe Bat's most obvious feature is the complicated shape of the top of the snout made of folds of fleshy skin, part of which is the shape of a horseshoe; and Disc-winged bats have a circular adhesive sucker at the base of the thumb. Unfortunately not all the names are so useful: Funnel-eared bats certainly have ears of that shape but so do some other species, and 'Evening' Bat could describe any bat. As for the Hog-nosed Bat – this, the smallest mammal, may have a distinctive snout yet is a delicate and attractive species (some even get a buzz out of calling it the bumblebee bat).

Just a flavour of the amazing world of bats...

Whilst unsuccessfully looking for the possibly extinct Pteralopex *fruit bat on the isolated Solomon Islands I did manage to study the Solomon Island Tube-nosed fruit bat. This bat has BIG eyes and flies below the canopy in the tropical forest where it is BLACK at night. Long tubes for nostrils pointing outwards at 45° help it locate fruit by smelling in a sort of stereo. It has yellow blotches all over the wings and ears which camouflage it in daytime as it hangs up in a tree like a bunch of leaves. Like so many tropical island bats, it is rare and threatened through habitat loss (logging!). An incredible bat!*

Bats in Britain

Here we are, over 3,000 miles from the equator, on the extreme edge of a big land mass, in a temperate climate and on an island. It is not surprising (see p. 12) that there are only 16 resident species, representing only 2 of the 18 bat families of the world. Ireland, even more remote, has only 7 recorded species. The rest of Europe has twice as many species as Britain but mainly from the same two families (see table below). In addition to our resident species, there have been odd records of Hoary Bat, Silver-haired Bat and Big Brown Bat from North America, the former a migratory species, the others imported accidentally with goods, and Northern Bat, Parti-coloured Bat and Savi's Pipistrelle, all species from mainland Europe.

FAMILY	BRITISH SPECIES	BRITISH RANGE AND STATUS	ADDITIONAL SPECIES IN REST OF EUROPE
Horseshoe bats (*Rhinolophidae*)	Greater Horseshoe (*Rhinolophus ferrum-equinum*)	S. Wales, S.W. England Becoming rare	Mediterranean Horseshoe (*R. euryale*)
	Lesser Horseshoe (*R. hipposideros*)	Wales, S.W. England, W. Ireland Decreasing in number	Blasius's Horseshoe (*R. blasii*) Mehely's Horseshoe (*R. mehelyi*)
Vesper bats (*Vespertilionidae*)			
	MYOTIS		
	Whiskered (*M. mystacinus*)	England, Wales and probably Ireland Widespread	Geoffroy's (*M. emarginatus*)
	Brandt's (*M. brandtii*)	Probably as above but rarer	Long-fingered (*M. capaccinii*)
	Natterer's (*M. nattereri*)	Widespread throughout	Lesser Daubenton's (*M. nathalinae*)
	Bechstein's (*M. bechsteinii*)	Parts of S. England Very rare	Pond (*M. dasycneme*)
	Mouse-eared (*M. myotis*)	S. Coast England Extinct in 1991	Lesser Mouse-eared (*M. blythi*)
	Daubenton's (*M. daubentonii*)	Widespread throughout	

FAMILY	BRITISH SPECIES	BRITISH RANGE AND STATUS	ADDITIONAL SPECIES IN REST OF EUROPE
NOCTULES, PIPISTRELLES AND ALLIES			
	Serotine (*Eptesicus serotinus*)	S. and E. England Widespread	Northern (*E. nilssonii*)
	Leisler's (*Nyctalus leisleri*)	S. and Central England and Ireland Rare in England	Greater Noctule (*N. lasiopterus*)
	Noctule (*N. noctula*)	Mainly England and Wales Widespread	Parti-coloured (*Vespertilio murinus*) (Vagrant in England)
	Pipistrelle 45 kHz (*Pipistrellus sp.*)	Widespread throughout	Kuhl's Pipistrelle (*P. kuhli*)
	Pipistrelle 55 kHz (*Pipistrellus sp.*)	Widespread throughout	Savi's Pipistrelle (*P. savii*)
	Nathusius' Pipistrelle (*P. nathusii*)	Breeding discovered in late 1990s. Limited distribution. Rare.	
LONG-EAREDS, ETC.			
	Barbastelle (*Barbastella barbastellus*)	Mainly S. and E. England, S. Wales Very rare	Schreiber's (*Miniopterus schreibersi*)
	Brown Long-eared (*Plecotus auritus*)	Widespread throughout	
	Grey long-eared (*P. austriacus*)	Parts of S. England Very rare	
Free-tailed bats (*Molossidae*)			European free-tailed (*Tadarida teniotis*)

Hoary Bat (*Lasarius cinereus*): there has been one Scottish record of this vagrant from N. America.

All the resident British species are found on the warm south coast of England; 9 or 10 are in the Midlands; but the cooler, more barren north tip of Scotland has only 2 or 3 species. The range of the different species is not only affected by the climate (which also affects their insect prey – all European bats are insectivorous), but also by the availability of roosting sites such as caves and holes in old trees and the different ways that farmland and woodland are managed, as this also affects insect diversity and density. Such reasons explain in part why some species are rare, some are thinly spread or have a patchy distribution yet others are widespread across their range. Pipistrelles, for instance, are found in most areas of Britain. They have adapted to roosting primarily in houses and even show a marked preference for modern buildings – a habitat that is not in short supply. Others, such as Bechstein's bat, roost in holes and crevices in old trees, often deep in woodland, and suitable places are becoming more difficult to find.

Bat identification is usually impossible until the bat is closely examined in the hand (and even then it can be difficult). Nevertheless you can sometimes get an idea of its identity (see overleaf). The chart includes the most commonly seen species, but remember that other species do occur and do look very similar. In fact some species are almost identical to others in their outward appearance, and there is no easy key for the bat enthusiast to use to identify a bat positively. The possibility of a few European species nipping across to Britain (e.g. Nathusius' Pipistrelle, Parti-coloured, Pond and Geoffroy's bats) must always be borne in mind and this further complicates identification. Practice and experience certainly helps and if you manage to identify common species, then the rarer ones will stand out as being different. The identification guide here (see p. 19) is designed with this in mind. Remember that it is illegal to disturb bats, and that you must have a licence to handle them.

Parti-coloured Bat.

Characteristics of commonly found bats

	FLIGHT; TIME SEEN	HABITATS
Pipistrelle	Small. Just above head height. Irregular twists and dives. Soon after sunset.	Around towns and villages. Large numbers in eaves of modern houses.
Daubenton's Bat	Medium size. Pale underparts. Low over water at all times (like a hovercraft). Seen when dark.	Still or slow-moving water.
Noctule	Large (size of a Swift) with narrow wings. Very high (above tops of trees) but with sudden dives to ground before regaining height. Covers great distances. Soon after sunset.	Often over water when feeding. Not in Ireland, few in Scotland.
Brown Long-eared Bat	Ears sometimes visible. Medium size: broad wings and slow flight, almost hovers at times. In amongst branches or low over ground. Emerges late.	Orchards, old parkland, woodland. Found in attics roosting in exposed positions. At night hangs up in shelters (porches, churches, barns).

Notes on confusing species (opposite page)
(i) Grey Long-eared Bat is a similar but rare species found on S. coast of England. Measure thumb length and tragus width.
(ii) Nathusius' Pipistrelle occurs rarely. Measure forearm and 5th finger. Also Pipistrelle is now split into two species, one echo-locates loudest at 45 kHz, the other at 55 kHz: the former has a black face mask ('bandit'), the latter has an all-brown face.
(iii) Brandt's Bat is very similar and occurs in similar range. Check shapes of male organ and 3rd upper pre-molar.

THE ROAD TO BAT IDENTIFICATION

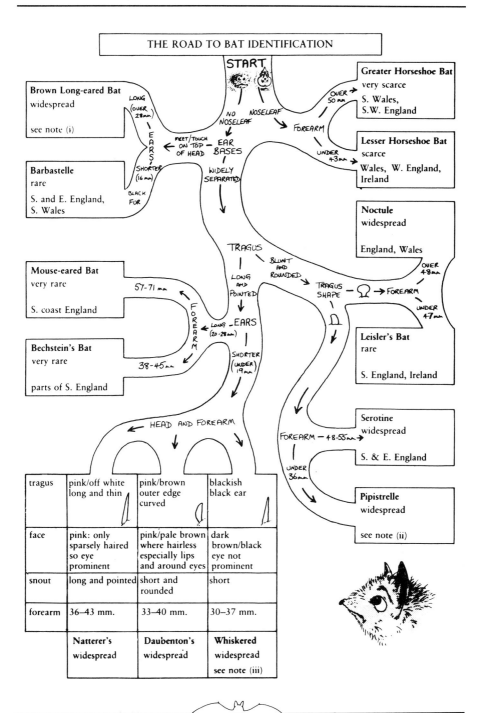

START

Brown Long-eared Bat
widespread

see note (i)

Barbastelle
rare

S. and E. England,
S. Wales

Greater Horseshoe Bat
very scarce

S. Wales,
S.W. England

Lesser Horseshoe Bat
scarce

Wales, W. England,
Ireland

Noctule
widespread

England, Wales

Mouse-eared Bat
very rare

S. coast England

Bechstein's Bat
very rare

parts of S. England

Leisler's Bat
rare

S. England, Ireland

Serotine
widespread

S. & E. England

Pipistrelle
widespread

see note (ii)

LONG (OVER 28mm) — EARS — SHORTER (16mm) — BLACK FUR

EAR BASES — MEET/TOUCH ON TOP OF HEAD / WIDELY SEPARATED

NO NOSELEAF / NOSELEAF — FOREARM — OVER 50mm / UNDER 43mm

TRAGUS — LONG AND POINTED / BLUNT AND ROUNDED — TRAGUS SHAPE — FOREARM — OVER 48mm / UNDER 47mm

57-71mm — FOREARM — 38-45mm

LONG EARS (20-28mm) — SHORTER (UNDER 19mm)

HEAD AND FOREARM

FOREARM — 48-55mm — UNDER 36mm

	pink/off white long and thin	pink/brown outer edge curved	blackish black ear
tragus			
face	pink: only sparsely haired so eye prominent	pink/pale brown where hairless especially lips and around eyes	dark brown/black eye not prominent
snout	long and pointed	short and rounded	short
forearm	36–43 mm.	33–40 mm.	30–37 mm.
	Natterer's widespread	**Daubenton's** widespread	**Whiskered** widespread see note (iii)

Lesser Horseshoe

Greater Horseshoe

Barbastelle

Serotine

Leisler's

Noctule

Brown Long-eared

Grey Long-eared

Pipistrelle

Daubenton's

Natterer's

Whiskered

Brandt's

Bechstein's

Mouse-eared

Bat bits – the structure

Sizing them up

At rest, bats bear a few superficial similarities to shrews or mice, but can easily be told from them. Bats, for instance, can hang by their toe-nails from rafters, whereas mice so far haven't managed this. In flight they look a little like birds, but few birds fly at night and none with the agile twists and jinks that bats perform. They are mammals and, like most mammals, have bodies covered in hair and suckle their young after giving birth.

When you first see a British bat, you are amazed at how small it is. The Pipistrelle is the smallest, with head and body only 1½ inches (4 cm.) long: it would fit snugly into a matchbox. Pipistrelles only weigh ⅕ oz. (4 or 5 g.) (equivalent to the weight of about 10 paperclips). Even the biggest bat is only 3 inches long (6–8 cm.) and weighs in at about an ounce (20–35 g.). Three contenders for the Biggest Bat in Britain title are the Noctule, Serotine and Greater Horseshoe bats and all are about the same size. A rank outsider takes the award, however: the Mouse-eared Bat which is a little bigger than them all . . . but unfortunately went extinct in 1991.

Generally female bats are slightly larger than males of the same species but there is plenty of size variation in both sexes.

Body hair

Quite a dense fur completely covers bats' bodies and helps their insulation. The hairs that make up this snug, made-to-measure fur coat look rather unusual when studied closely under a microscope. Each hair is coated in a layer of fine scales giving a distinctive appearance like a stack of flower-pots.

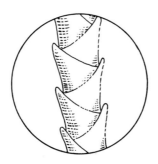

Hair (Myotis) under the microscope.

The hairs are quite long in comparison with the size of the body, and this makes bats look bulkier than they really are. A naked bat would look very thin indeed – and quite embarrassed. A Pipistrelle, for instance, is only ½ inch (10 mm.) from front to back, yet it has hair over ½ inch (10 mm.) long, making it look plump and cuddly. The slow-flying Long-eared Bat has a coat that is very fluffed up, whereas that of the fast-flying Noctule is smooth, sleek and glossy.

The colour of the coat differs for each species, but generally they are all some shade of grey, brown or black above and off-white, buff or brown below. None of the British bats has the stripes or patches seen in some tropical species. The individual hairs often have three colours along their length, so the overall impression of the colour can look different if the fur is smoothed down or fluffed up or if viewed from a different angle. Pipistrelles have hair on their upper-parts which is usually black-rooted, pale buff in the middle and brown on the tips.

Bats are very attached to their fur coats and look after them with regular and careful grooming; they keep themselves meticulously clean. They hang by one foot and use the claws of the other foot as a comb. In this way they ensure that their fur is kept spotless and in good condition. They moult every year, so old, worn hairs are replaced by new ones. Young bats have a much greyer coat than adults and it is often more downy, too. After a few months this colour difference fades and they look increasingly like adults.

Wings

Bats have bone structures in their hands almost identical to man's but with very long, thin fingers, each almost as long as the body. The fingers are joined with a very elastic membrane of brown or black almost hairless skin which is

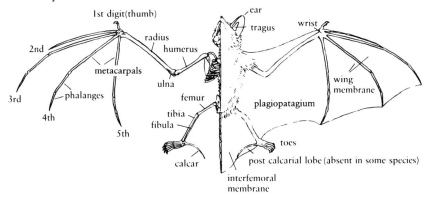

Bat structure.

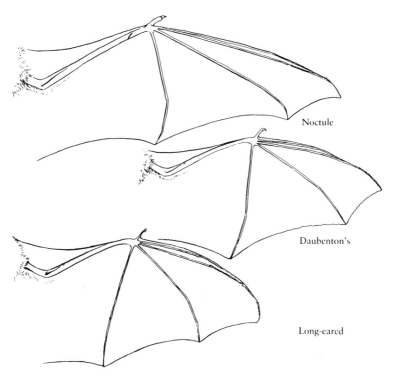

Noctule

Daubenton's

Long-eared

Different wing shapes have evolved for varying life styles.

also attached to their sides and back legs. It looks as if all they have to do is to spread their fingers, beat their arms up and down and off they go, but actually it takes a lot of energy and hard work to fly so they usually launch from a high point and gain a bit of speed as they fall down before they are properly flying (a sort of bump-start). Slight flexing of a finger will alter the wing shape and no end of aero-bat-ics are then possible; bats are far more manoeuvrable than even the most agile bird. Unlike the feathers on a bird's wing, the bat's membrane allows no air to pass through, so they can execute very sharp turns without the 'drifting' experienced by birds. Bird wing feathers are replaced annually – very necessary, as they get worn out. The membrane of a bat's wing is living tissue and so small holes caused perhaps by pilot-error (such as flying too close to a tree branch) will heal over with pink scar tissue. Large holes will not close up but just heal at the edges and, as long as there is still enough surface area, then the bat continues to fly.

Different wing shapes have different uses. Noctules have a long, thin wing

that is ideal for fast flight and they can whizz along at 30 m.p.h. (50 k.p.h.), whereas Long-eared bats have broad wings, which enable them to fly very slowly and even hover. Daubenton's bats have a medium wing and cruise along at 10–15 m.p.h. (16–25 k.p.h.)

Tail and back legs – the blunt end
Although a bat's tail is almost as long as its body, it is not very easy to see because it is completely enclosed in a membrane of skin joining it to the back legs. In addition it curls its tail under its body at rest, tucking it out of sight. The membrane would make it very difficult for a bat to run around on the ground – a bit like taking part in a sack race – but in the air it seems to be useful as an air brake, probably helping direction changes; best of all, it is a useful place to tuck insects temporarily when your hands are full with flying along. Extra stiffening of the trailing edge of the tail membrane is provided by a thin sliver of cartilage called the 'calcar', which is attached to the heel. The legs are designed so that the feet can be pointed backwards or sideways, which helps when scrambling about inside narrow roosting places and also makes hanging more comfortable from perches. Yes, at rest bats do hang from rafters in attics or crevices on a cave roof, for instance. You may have wondered whether the blood rushes to the bat's head as it hangs: it's a very good question and I hear that the bats are just as puzzled about why the blood doesn't drain from our heads when we get out of bed in the morning. You may have wondered how bats can go to sleep when hanging upside down from a perch without relaxing their grip and dropping off. The answer lies in the cunning arrangement of tendons in the toes. The toes and claws on each foot act rather like grappling irons. The weight of the bat hanging below keeps the

toes in a clenched position and the heavier the bat then the firmer is the grip. The claws are quite small but very sharp and will grip the smallest of crevices on an apparently smooth surface.

In this way bats will find a suitable resting place well out of the way of any predator, being high up in the roof of a building or cave. They point head downwards, hanging free just by their toes, particularly when taking a short rest at night. During the day, however, many move into a more protected position, perhaps where two roof timbers meet or maybe deep in a narrow crevice. In such positions their undersides are in contact with the support and they also grip it with the tiny claws on their thumbs. If the crevice happens to be a horizontal slot then the bats will roost horizontally – they do not *have* to hang downwards. Bats in a cluster hang onto those above. Underneath that cuddly cushion of bats there is one poor bat with a number of friends to support – the rest are just hangers-on!

Head – the sharp end

Daubenton's.

Many species differ in the shape and size of the ear, length of snout, colour of bare skin and amount of fur cover on the face.

Teeth: baby bats have milk teeth from birth but grow permanent teeth after a couple of weeks. The milk teeth are very sharp and slightly hooked and

Brown Long-eared: skull and front view of teeth.

are probably used for getting a better grip on the mother, particularly when she is flying around with the baby slung beneath her. The permanent teeth are designed for insects: the cheek teeth (molars) have 'W' shaped tips which cut up and crush insect food and the canines are fairly long and pointed, so are handy for gripping a struggling insect. The front teeth (incisors) are very small and only just visible through a magnifying glass. This means that bats cannot bite chunks off their food but have to chew away at large insects using the side of the mouth with the insect protruding like a cigar. It also means that bats have rather a toothless grin.

The senses
Sight: 'As blind as a bat' is a non-sense. All bats can see perfectly well but their eyes seem best suited for low light levels. Their eyes cannot distinguish colour – but that would be of little use anyway to a night-flying animal. It is important for bats to be able to tell if it is dark enough to venture out of their roost sites (places where bats hang out during the day) and also for them to see their way around inside. Eyesight is probably important, too, for orientation so that they can find their roost sites again after a night of feeding. Some species may rely more heavily on eyesight than others – the Long-eared Bat, for instance, has relatively large eyes.

Smell: do bats smell? Yes, with both nostrils. We really do not know how important the sense of smell is to our bats but the few hints we get indicate that it could be very important indeed. Some species, particularly tropical bats, have scent glands on the face, under the base of the tail and even on the chest. The scent may not be 'Love in a Mist' but it means a great deal to other bats, and secretions from the glands are used to mark roosting sites as well as each other. Mothers may well use scent to identify their youngsters from all the others in a nursery roost (see p. 46). Many of the scents cannot be detected by mere humans, but sometimes you may notice a musky smell. One Pipistrelle I

handled gave off liberal amounts of this odour onto my fingers and everything I touched soon had the same smell. It may drive other Pipistrelles wild with passion but all I got was some very funny looks and plenty of space when I went into the local pub for an after-batting drink. To me it is not unpleasant, just distinctly batty.

Hearing: bats' hearing is very sensitive, but most sensitive to sounds of a higher pitch than we can hear. Many deep notes may not be clearly heard by most bats but a dog-whistle would be obvious. This does mean that extra special care is needed in areas where bats are roosting. The noises of scraping of a shoe on gravel, the rustle of a nylon jacket and even whispering

SSSSSHH!!
we don't want to wake
him up ……

(especially 'S' and 'T' sounds) contain high frequency parts and these will disturb bats. This warning system gives the bats a good measure of protection but they will not tolerate continued disturbance and will move out. It is against the law to disturb bats at roost so remember to be quiet ultrasonically when anywhere nearby.

Echo-location – what makes bats 'tick'

This very clever system enables bats to find their way around in the dark and to pinpoint the whereabouts of flying insects. Very simply, it involves the bat giving out a short, loud shout and carefully listening to all the echoes as the sound bounces back from buildings, trees, the ground, insects and anything else in the area. The echo will come back almost immediately from close objects but will take longer to return from more distant things. It will also be louder from close objects. The echoes from a solid concrete wall will be 'clearer' than those received from waving leaves on a tree. The bat can,

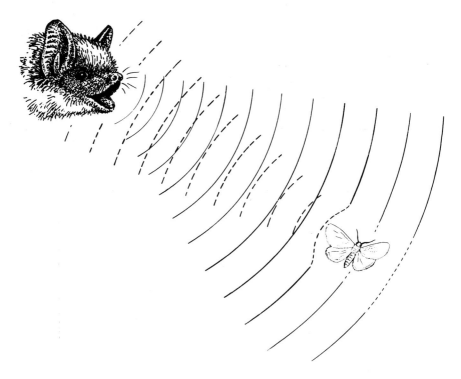

Echo-location.

therefore, build up a picture of the position and distance of objects around it and also learn something of their texture. We see scenes as the pattern of light reflected from objects; bats 'see' by interpreting patterns of sounds echoing from their surroundings. To get more information the bats give out a number of shouts, about ten every second, and listen to the series of echoes. If an echo seems to come from a slightly different direction relative to the bat after each call then it is a moving object and may be an insect – food.

In practice the calls are very complex and made up of many different sounds of different frequencies. Some parts of a call give information about how fast an insect is moving and other parts give a good idea of the size and substance of the object. It is a very sensitive system and can easily 'see' very small insects or fine wires in pitch-black conditions. Echo-location calls are often very loud, yet we cannot hear them, because they are usually of frequencies above our range. It is now possible to buy electronic 'bat detectors' which pick up these inaudible calls and convert them into a sound that we can hear. This has made it much easier for bat workers to find bats and discover more about their interesting life styles. Although most species give out calls that sound like rapid clicks on the detector (each click being a single shout) there are differences between each species. Some bats call very rapidly, others more slowly, some loudly and others more softly; different species use different frequency calls. The detector can therefore be used to identify species but it does take a lot of practice. Some are easy: the Noctule gives a slow 'chonk' a few times a second. At the height it flies there is little danger of colliding with anything so it calls infrequently, but the calls are very loud so that it can still hear the echoes that have a long way to travel. Daubenton's Bat gives out a very rapid and regular series of clicks (about 13 a second). It flies very close to water and a short pause in the calls might cause temporary 'blindness' and a dunking. When an insect is detected, the bat closes in and the calls become faster and faster until they become a buzz at the point of contact. This enables the bat to detect any change in direction of the insect and to assess accurately its range as it rapidly approaches.

There are always some exceptions. The Horseshoe Bat does not shout the calls out through its mouth but sends the sounds through its peculiarly shaped nose. The strangely shaped snout (noseleaf) probably aids the directing of the sounds. You may think that the calls would sound a bit odd – rather like someone sneezing very rapidly. In fact when you hear it on the bat detector, it is a most beautiful sound – a rich, continuous, bubbling warble of notes. Another exception is Long-eared bats, which do not shout out their echo-location calls, but whisper them. Their large ears, no doubt, can pick up the faint echoes. Some moths can hear bats' calls and keep out of the way

Moth avoiding capture on hearing approaching Natterer's Bat.

when bats are hunting, but it has been suggested that they cannot hear the whispers of the Long-eared Bat which then catches these moths that the other bats miss. There are probably many other reasons for the quiet calls of this bat yet to be discovered. Barbastelles and Natterer's bats have relatively large ears and also call fairly quietly.

There are many unanswered questions about the complex echo-location system of bats. The function of the tragus (inner ear) remains much of a mystery, for instance. Bats are never confused by echoes from other bats but they certainly listen to them. Possibly they learn which bats are feeding successfully and then join in. Intercommunication between bats by high frequency calls is very likely but little is yet known. As you can see, there remains a wealth of interesting research to be carried out in this fascinating world of sound.

Other sounds

Apart from their high frequency calls, bats make audible sounds as well, especially chattering inside roost sites. The purpose of such behaviour remains a mystery. Sometimes this continues for most of the day, yet at other times there is no sound at all. Pipistrelle roosts in summer are good places to hear this occasional chattering; other species such as Noctules, Daubenton's and Whiskered bats are often very noisy at summer roosts, too. Nearer dusk the hubbub increases as the excitement at the roost mounts. There may also be a buzzing sound like a fly trapped in a matchbox. This is usually a sign that the bats have been disturbed. Baby bats have a very high pitched, but audible, squeak which attracts the mother's attention, often over considerable distances. I was given a half-sized baby Pipistrelle that had been found under a roost site. I went straight back to the site to return the youngster, but the adults had already flown off to feed. I put the baby on the wall just below the entrance hole and it quickly scrambled back inside and began squeaking very loudly. Immediately two adult Pipistrelles came flying back, popped in the hole and the squeaking stopped. These bats had been nowhere in sight and almost pushed past me to get to the youngster.

Bat detectors

Bats give out high frequency shouts ('ultrasounds') all the time they are flying. Each shout lasts only a few hundredths of a second and most calls during that time sweep down from very high to lower frequencies - almost down to human hearing range. Bat detectors are electronic devices that can pick up these shouts and convert them into a sound we can hear. There are two different designs. A detector widely used to identify bats as they fly past is a heterodyne type and the sounds come out as a series of clicks, clonks or warbles. Warbles are from Horseshoe Bats, and by tuning the detector we can tell which species. Clonks are from Noctules, Leisler's and Serotine bats. These are well separated calls and often sound like 'shop'. They are also very loud. The clicks are from the other species which initially all sound similar, but with practice can be distinguished by listening to the quality, spacing, volume and sharpness of the clicks. Pipistrelles always sound a bit wet and 'slappy'. Long-eared Bats are very quiet and issue a very sharp series of clicks. The new species of Pipistrelle in Britain was first distinguished by listening to the calls on a detector - one species is loudest when the detector is tuned to 45 kiloHertz (kHz), the other at 55 kHz. When bats are about to catch an insect their shouts speed up and sound like a 'raspberry' on the detector - useful for working out what the bats are doing.

The other detector type uses time expansion. Basically it 'records' a short part of a passing bat's calls, then plays it back slowly. Slowing it lowers the frequency down into the audible range for humans, and through headphones it sounds like the mournful cries of whales. The great advantage is that the information can be played back through a sound analysis program on a PC. Each shout is then fully analysed as a sonogram showing frequency range, length of call, call spacings and intensity. Different species can then be told apart.

Detectors are still evolving. Their prices vary from under £50 for a make-it-yourself kit to over £1000 for one that does everything but make the tea. Information on suppliers and advice can be obtained from your local Bat Group or the Bat Conservation Trust.

Bat grub

Although one third of bat species eat fruit, about two thirds of the bat species of the world are insectivorous, and this includes all the British and European species. In Britain alone there are over 20,000 species of insect so the bats seem spoilt for choice, but there are a number of limitations to their diet. Day-flying butterflies and wasps and terrestrial insects are caught infrequently, as bats are primarily aerial and night-time feeders (Horseshoe, Mouse-eared and some other bats, however, do land on the ground at times to take beetles). Some insects are poisonous or distasteful and so must be avoided. There are more insects of greater variety in the warmer south of Britain than in the north and this limit to their diet probably affects the distribution of some species. Bats have physical limitations to their diets: for instance, a small Pipistrelle would be unable to capture and eat a large flying beetle which might be almost as big as itself so it concentrates on smaller, soft-bodied insects. The large Noctule on the other hand has strong teeth and jaws which are ideally designed for crunching up big beetles.

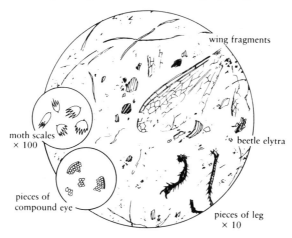

Food remnants as seen under the microscope.

The diet
Discovering which insects are taken is not easy. A few species (e.g. Horseshoes and Long-eared bats) take back larger snacks to eat at the roosting place, and discarded bits of food (insect wings, legs, etc.) litter the ground in a pile underneath. Such pieces are quite easy to identify. Small

insects, though, are eaten whole (wrappings and all) and other bat species eat their insects in flight. Many insect remains can still be identified because they come through the bat's digestive system and form the droppings, which can be collected from under a roost. Careful examination of the droppings spread out on a glass slide under the microscope will show up the indigestible parts of insects such as legs, wings, scales, compound eyes and body cases, all ground up very finely. Trying to identify the insect species from this jumble of parts is an interesting challenge, a sort of 'Build your own beetle. Only 986 parts. No plans or glue provided.' It is easier if comparisons can be made with identified insects that have been collected from the area where the bats are feeding. Very soft-bodied or small insects leave few traces so may be easily missed but many of the larger prey items can be identified. This method of analysis can also show how the diet changes during the summer as different insects emerge and others die off.

Feeding places
Bats congregate where insects are abundant, and this depends upon the type of vegetation and amount of shelter. Insects accumulate in sheltered areas such as along the edges of woodland, by tall hedges and in enclosed gardens and churchyards. If there is a variety of vegetation there will be a variety of insects; some types of plants or trees are especially attractive – honeysuckle is just one example; damp areas such as river edges will have large numbers of insects. When bats emerge from their roost sites they generally follow a main flight path – an interesting point because they only emerge at night from the roost in small numbers and the first ones to come out are often well out of sight before the next lot emerge, yet they follow precisely the same aerial path. Once away from the roost area individuals turn off from the main flight path and go to their own favourite feeding areas. In this way a large roost will be dispersed over a wide area and there is not so much feeding competition. Some well studied species such as Noctules and Pipistrelles have been shown to have regular flight paths within a feeding area, always keeping to specified boundaries. One Noctule I watched used a telephone wire stretched across a canal as one boundary edge, a lock as another and the edges of the canal as the other two. It repeatedly hunted insects within this area for twenty minutes, turning sharply on reaching a boundary line. The time any bat spends in a feeding area obviously depends on its success, and eventually the bat will move to other sites. Insects are not active all night but a lot are flying in the first two hours after sunset and there is another burst of activity just before dawn. In between these times insects are thin on the ground – well, thin in the air, anyway. Bats tend to feed at these active times. Another factor that affects

insect numbers is temperature: when it drops below 10°C then there is a noticeable decrease in the number of active insects; rain causes many insects to seek shelter; moonlight has a surprising effect – the catches of moths at light-traps drop dramatically on moonlit nights. To recap, then, fat bats are found within two hours after sunset on warm, calm, overcast nights in summer near sheltered places with good varieties of vegetation.

The art of catching insects in flight

Finding insects is primarily achieved by using ultrasonic echo-location, as described before (see p. 28). Eyesight is probably used as an aid in locating suitable feeding areas and the bats' sensitive hearing may also be used as many insects fly noisily. Insects vary in size, speed of flight, flight movements and wing beats and all these features can be detected by the bats' echo-

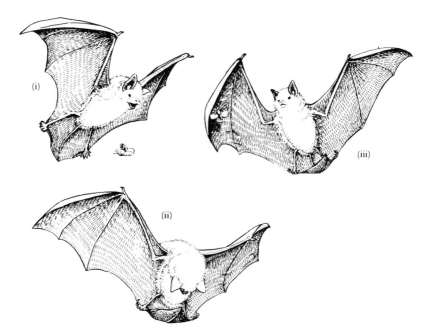

Techniques used by bats for capturing flying insect prey. Insects, particularly small ones, are usually caught directly in the mouth. Larger ones may be scooped out of the air by the tail membrane (i) before being transferred to the mouth (ii). Should the insect take evasive action, the bat may gather it with its wing and flick the prey towards the head, either to be grasped directly or held initially in the tail membrane (iii).

location system. It is likely that, using this information, bats can select favoured foods amongst the soup of insects in front of them. The next problem is to catch the insect. It would seem natural for us to reach out with a hand and grab it when it was within reach, but since bats are flying with their hands, such an action would quickly bring about their downfall. They will use a wing at times to deflect an insect towards the mouth, but usually the bat will fly close to its prey and catch it using a combination of its mouth and its tail membrane which it uses as a catching-basket-cum-temporary-holding-place in which to push the insect with vigorous shovings of the head whilst obtaining a better grip with the mouth.

Different species have different feeding strategies. The Long-eared Bat has broad wings which enable it to fly slowly and even hover; it can fly amongst tree branches, twisting and turning and plucking insects from the foliage. Noctules, with long thin wings, fly fast and stay up high patrolling over a wide area until they detect a big juicy moth, beetle or grasshopper; they then plunge down on it in a spectacular dive before returning to patrol. Daubenton's bats have quite a shallow, quivering wing-beat and they fly most of the time very close to the surface of water rather like a hovercraft and catch insects from the surface with their mouths or even their specially adapted large feet. Though such different feeding methods mean less competition between bat species for food, there is a sharing of prey items, of course; bats will take other insects if the chance arises.

Daubenton's Bat hunting caddis fly over water.

Drink

Bats obtain moisture from the juicy insides of insects, but they do need to drink as well. They do so by swooping low over the surface of water and snatching a sip in flight. Any water will do – garden ponds, lakes or canals. Some are seen sipping from outdoor swimming pools, so perhaps they like their water chlorinated. In tunnels and caves they lap droplets of water from the roof whilst resting: this water would be full of dissolved minerals and very beneficial.

A snack or a meal?

The activities of bats at night are still not fully known. Although many species will be away from the day-roost for much of the night they are not necessarily flying all the time and some are known to have separate night-time roosts. Nor are they feeding all the time they are flying — they might be courting or finding a new roost site. Nevertheless they do eat an enormous number of insects when the chance arises, as can be seen by re-weighing a bat when it returns to its roost. Sometimes their little stomachs are bulging

with insects, and they have increased their body weight by 25%. The food remains pass quickly through the digestive system so the measured weight increase is only a proportion of the food caught. As the weight of an insect is so minute, the

numbers caught are staggering. With over 5,000 gnats being equivalent in weight to one Pipistrelle 500 gnats would provide a mere 10% weight increase – fairly average for this species. A roost of 100 Pipistrelles will eat over 1½ million gnats in a month: some estimate that it may be nearer 9 million. Many insects consumed are harmful ones – woodworm, death-watch beetle, blood-sucking mosquitoes and the like; so bats are doing us a favour, though they receive scant recognition for it.

Brown Long-eared Bat.

Bats and pats

Internal parasites in cattle are controlled by drugs such as Ivermectin. Unfortunately, this comes out of the animal in the cow pats and carries on working, killing dung beetles and other insects that live by the motto 'waste not, want not'.

These insects are a main food source of some bats such as horseshoes and serotines which hunt around cow pastures. Banning its use in some batty areas has begun to help the beleaguered bats. A pat on the back for those involved.

Bats and their food

Prey items (MAIN ITEMS IN BOLD, IF KNOWN)

Greater Horseshoe	Moths (especially Noctuids), **beetles** (cockchafer, dor and scavenger), caddis, *Diptera* (e.g. cranefly)
Lesser Horseshoe	Small moths, *Diptera* (e.g. **cranefly**), small beetles, lacewings
Whiskered bat	Mayfly, small moths, *Diptera* (e.g. cranefly)
Natterer's bat	*Diptera*, moths, caddis
Bechstein's bat	Moths
Mouse-eared bat	Large moths and beetles
Daubenton's bat	**Caddis**, *Diptera* (especially **chironomids**), moths, beetles, mayflies, water boatman
Serotine	Beetles (especially cockchafer), large moths
Leisler's bat	Moths, beetles, caddis, *Diptera* (e.g. dung-fly)
Noctule	**Beetles** (especially cockchafer and dor), crickets, moths
Pipistrelle	**Diptera**, caddis, moths, may flies, lacewings
Barbastelle	*Diptera*
Brown Long-eared bat	**Moths** (especially Noctuids), cranefly, caddis, beetles (especially scarab), *Diptera* (especially midges)

This list of prey items is incomplete; little work has been carried out on the foods of many species in Britain.

Diptera are flies, midges, mosquitoes and gnats.

Torpidity and hibernation

In the tropics there is a wealth of food for bats throughout much of the year and the temperature stays high at all times. In temperate areas the picture is very different. The cold weather in winter limits the numbers of active insects so there is little available food for our insectivorous bats – and just at a time when they could really benefit from a good meal to warm them up and stop their teeth from chattering. Even in summer the weather conditions can alter dramatically and strong winds, cold or rain at night keep insects under shelter. Such weather can last for many days, but bats survive due to a remarkable energy-saving strategy – they can become torpid. This involves cooling down to approximately the same temperature as the surroundings, by a slowing-down of the heart beat, breathing and other body systems. The colder it becomes outside, the colder become the bats as their body systems get slower and slower and so save more and more energy, until they are just ticking over. They can stay in this state for many weeks if necessary. They look as if they are in a very deep sleep, but can be aroused by a change of temperature, sudden noise or when dusk falls. As they wake up they begin to warm up, the heart beats more quickly, breathing gets faster and they soon begin to shiver, a process which is thought to help the warming-up process. They usually warm up about 1°C each minute or two, so it is often at least 15 minutes before they are back at active temperature again, and only then can they fly (see p. 42). Such an energy-saving system is very useful as it means that the energy generated from a meal can be made to last longer. Bats will save energy by going torpid in daytime even when the weather is not unpleasant.

During winter, temperatures become very low and there are few opportunities to feed. Many insect-eating birds migrate to warmer areas where the food is abundant and, although some bats have been shown to migrate, the temperate species survive the winter by hibernating – a torpid state which lasts on and off from October to April. In late summer and autumn they build up fat deposits in their bodies which act as their major fuel supply for the lean months ahead, some increasing their body weights by up to 35%. Hibernation is quite a complicated affair, since bats need to become active periodically during the winter. This is because the temperature conditions are always changing so they may need to change to a new hibernation site – not too cold or they suffer, and not too warm or their bodies will be unable to cool down enough, and will use a lot of their stored fat in keeping their bodies running at this high temperature. They also need to use such periods of activity to get rid of waste products and to drink. The humidity in the hibernation site (hibernaculum) is very important because bats soon dehydrate unless the site is humid enough. The arousal procedure uses up a large amount of the stored fat as fuel to make the bats warm again; they have only a limited quantity of fat to last all winter – some storing enough to enable them to become active only 4 or 5 times. Many stay in hibernation for only a few weeks at a time and, if the opportunity arises, will feed before returning to hibernation. Bats may sometimes even be seen feeding in daytime in winter.

Hibernacula tend to be humid, be well protected from extremes of cold or hot and be fairly inaccessible to predators. Typical examples are caves, mines and cavity walls of houses. Stone walls and tree holes are also used. A few species hang in exposed positions from the roofs of caves or tunnels, such as Horseshoe bats, which wrap their wings around their bodies like cloaks. Others, such as Daubenton's and Natterer's, tuck deep into crevices. Some cluster together, others remain apart. Temperatures of 0°–15°C are sought, the colder sites being used as winter progresses. In these cold conditions the heart beat may slow down to 25 beats a minute (it is 1,000 beats a minute when flying). Each bat will know a number of hibernacula so that it can

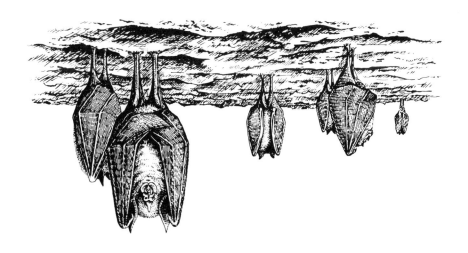

Greater Horseshoe bats hibernating.

choose the one with the best conditions and many of these may be traditional sites used every year. One tunnel that I visit is inhabited by a few Barbastelles – but only after a very sharp frost when they probably move out of more exposed sites such as trees to enter the more protected tunnel when the cold becomes too great – a natural safety mechanism wakes them up.

Whilst hibernating, bats are extremely vulnerable, because it takes them such a long time to become active. Nevertheless they are not entirely helpless and when disturbed can open their mouths and make a harsh rasping noise as a warning. Their feet can also move a little and seek a better foothold. They are easily disturbed by noise and lights and will begin to use up some of their valuable fat reserves as they begin to wake up. Hibernation sites should, therefore, be free from disturbance.

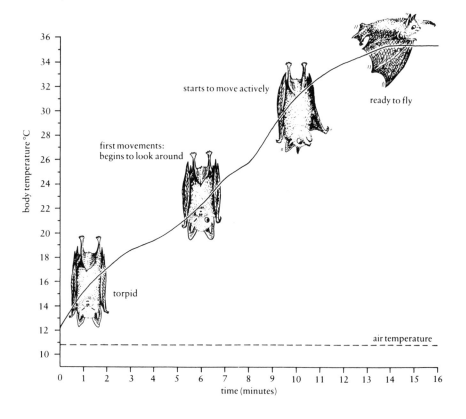

Torpid Pipistrelle 1/4/84 – body temperature increase on arousal.

By early spring the fat reserves are nearly all used up. This is a critical time because bats must feed or starve. Poor spring weather could result in many bats dying of starvation, particularly those that failed to put on much fat the previous autumn.

Activity

That's a laugh. In winter bats are deep in hibernation; they may rouse every now and again but soon return to that blissful state. This goes on for four or five months. In spring it's not much better. On warm days they may become active at dusk and go out to have a feed but usually only for a short while then it's straight back to the roost site to become torpid for the rest of the night, and stay torpid for much of the day as well. In late spring and in summer there are signs of life at last. They feed most nights but not continuously and after a few hours find somewhere quiet to have a rest — no point in over-taxing oneself. During the long summer days the time is spent snoozing in the roost sites. Chattering can be heard at some roosts — it's probably the bats talking in their sleep. In autumn the cooler weather means that they become torpid for longer periods. There is still some activity at night time but it gradually decreases as winter approaches.

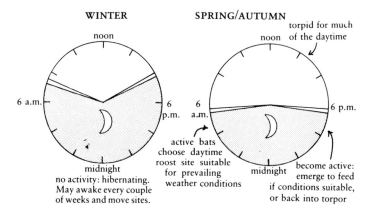

WINTER

noon

6 a.m.

6 p.m.

midnight

no activity: hibernating.
May awake every couple
of weeks and move sites.

SPRING/AUTUMN

torpid for much
of the daytime

noon

6
a.m.

6
p.m.

6 p.m.

active bats
choose daytime
roost site suitable
for prevailing
weather conditions

midnight

become active:
emerge to feed
if conditions suitable,
or back into torpor

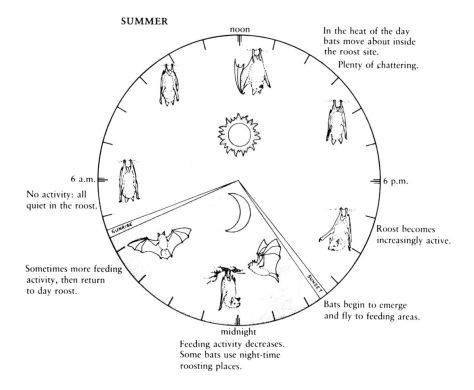

SUMMER

noon

In the heat of the day
bats move about inside
the roost site.

Plenty of chattering.

6 a.m.

No activity: all
quiet in the roost.

6 p.m.

GUNRISE

SUNSET

Roost becomes
increasingly active.

Sometimes more feeding
activity, then return
to day roost.

Bats begin to emerge
and fly to feeding areas.

midnight

Feeding activity decreases.
Some bats use night-time
roosting places.

A day in the life of a bat.

Breeding and rearing young

The sex lives and breeding habits of bats vary around the world. Some perform amazing displays and rituals before mating; pregnancies vary considerably in extent, and though most produce one, some produce up to three or even possibly four young. There is some variation in breeding behaviour of the European species, but a general pattern is followed. They mate in autumn and winter: active males seem keen to mate indiscriminately with any other bat of the same species that they encounter – females that may have just mated with another bat, torpid females and sometimes they even approach other males. It is not always easy to see when bats are mating, as many species form tightly packed clusters which make it impossible to see if a pair is mating in the middle of it or whether the whole cluster is just one big orgy. Usually, however, mating takes place away from big clusters. Even when a 'pair' of bats hang away from the others all may not be what it seems. I closely watched such a pair of Daubenton's bats which seemed to be mating – one hanging from a tunnel roof and the other tightly embracing the first in typical mating posture. Both were marked with wing clips and, on reading the serial numbers, I was amazed to find that they were both females. On a second occasion another pair was in an identical position but I wasn't to be fooled twice, so, after noticing that there were no pelvic movements, I carefully lifted off the uppermost bat and – yes, they were actually mating and the male was a bit put out by my intrusion!

Fertilization does not occur immediately after mating but is delayed until spring. The female carries the live male sperm in her body all winter then, after the rigours of hibernation, she ovulates and fertilization occurs, a feature of reproductive biology unique to bats. Schreiber's Bat of southern Europe (also found in tropical areas of Africa and Asia) does it a bit differently: the egg is fertilized after mating but the development is delayed until spring.

In spring the embryo begins to develop, but at a rate which is dependent upon food and temperature: when it is cold the females become torpid and development is dramatically slowed, so lengthening pregnancy. As the weather improves the females start to select roosting places that will be very warm in daytime and so speed up the development of the unborn young. At this time the females roost in single-sex groups and it is into these groups that the babies are born in June and July. These nursery colonies may contain many hundreds of females with their babies, so become quite noisy and busy places. A female produces only one baby a year but a few species such as

Noctule and Pipistrelle occasionally produce twins in some parts of Europe. During the birth the mother bats rely heavily on their tail membranes to hold the emerging youngsters and some females reverse themselves and hang from their thumbs so as to facilitate the birth, giving birth downwards with the aid of gravity. The baby bat then crawls up the underside of the mother to suckle on one of her two teats, situated one on each side of her chest. The mother protects and holds the baby by covering it with one of her wings. The young are quite hefty at birth, being about a quarter of the mother's weight, and must have been a strain to carry about prior to birth. The numbers of male and female babies are approximately equal.

The young are naked, blind and pink, but after a few days soft, dark grey hair begins to grow and the eyes are open after about a week. With mother's milk as daily food the young quickly grow. Initially they have 'milk' teeth, simple teeth with slight hooks, which the babies use to cling to their mothers in addition to the grip of the toes and thumbs. A good grip is essential because the mothers do carry their babies around with them at times, such as when changing roosting site. After a couple of weeks these first teeth are lost as the permanent teeth grow. During the night the mothers leave their young tucked into crevices or hanging in the roost site and go out to feed; but they soon return to suckle them, identifying their own babies by their high pitched squeaks and also by smell.

After three weeks the young are almost full size and some even fly out with

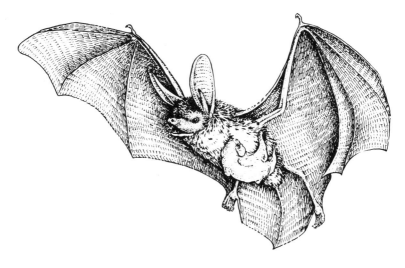

Female Bechstein's Bat carrying baby.

the adults. Milk is still provided for a few more weeks until the juveniles can catch their own insects. By August the offspring are almost independent but move around with adults, doubtlessly learning the locations of roosts and feeding areas and improving their skills as aerial insectivores. Bats are not usually sexually mature until in their second year and some, such as the Greater Horseshoe Bat, cannot breed before they are at least three or four years old. In the summer nursery colonies some adult females do not produce young – they may be infertile, have failed to mate successfully or perhaps have lost their unborn baby at an early stage. Bearing a youngster is quite a physical strain which may affect a bat throughout the rest of the year. After the birth the female must quickly regain her strength and build up fat reserves ready for hibernation. Poor feeding in early autumn due to bad weather could leave whole groups of females with insufficient fat to take them safely through winter; they may survive but probably lose their unborn youngsters. Even in summer the females have to feed regularly to produce the milk for the babies and a spell of poor weather results in no milk and death for the hungry youngsters.

Dear Diary

February 5th. *Dropped off on 2nd Jan, and didn't wake up until today. Felt a bit peckish so nipped out for a snack but little on the menu.*

March 12th. *Time to get up. Feels really spring-like. Plenty of mosquitoes flying: it's good to get fresh food again.*

April 8th. *This winter retreat seems a bit chilly now. Went out house-hunting without much success. Saw a nice 4-bedroomed house but it was too draughty.*

May 16th. *Bumped into a whole load of friends I knew from last year. They invited me back to their house and have put me up. The food is excellent. By the way: I'm pregnant. (Daren't tell Mum; I've no idea who the father was.)*

June 20th. *Have just produced the best looking baby boy-bat around here. He is gorgeous – just like his Mum.*

July 1st. *That baby wants feeding all the time. Never get a minute's rest. He is crying now. Lost him today: he went wandering off into the attic. Didn't know he was there until we heard the people who live below scream.*

August 26th. *Today some distant relatives dropped in. Hadn't seen them for years. Everyone is getting excited at present: they are all starting to hunt for*

The bat year.

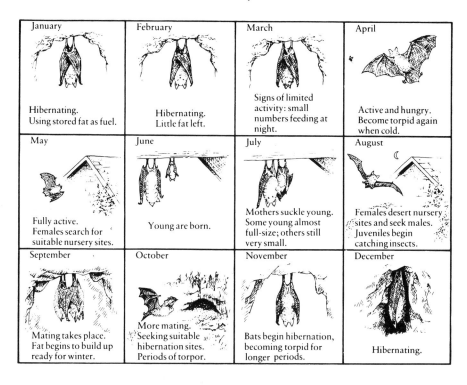

January	**February**	**March**	**April**
Hibernating. Using stored fat as fuel.	Hibernating. Little fat left.	Signs of limited activity: small numbers feeding at night.	Active and hungry. Become torpid again when cold.
May	**June**	**July**	**August**
Fully active. Females search for suitable nursery sites.	Young are born.	Mothers suckle young. Some young almost full-size; others still very small.	Females desert nursery sites and seek males. Juveniles begin catching insects.
September	**October**	**November**	**December**
Mating takes place. Fat begins to build up ready for winter.	More mating. Seeking suitable hibernation sites. Periods of torpor.	Bats begin hibernation, becoming torpid for longer periods.	Hibernating.

boyfriends again. Baby is now almost as big as me and he is a terrible handful. The youth of today never do as they are told.

September 10th. *I've found my mate. A real he-bat. He said he wanted to wrap his plagiopatagium around me!*

September 11th. *The little rat of a bat deserted me.*

October 15th. *Beginning to feel the cold a bit; I'm not as young as I was. I've really put on weight but I'm not that bothered; I'll soon lose it in spring.*

November 25th. *Found a perfect house for winter. A nice little place out in the country. I've always liked the country. Anyway, there is a perfect crevice inside the chimney stack.*

December 25th. *Some idiot came sliding down the chimney and woke me up. Ah well, it will soon be spring.*

Social structures

Bats are social animals, and members of a species will gather together, sometimes in their hundreds. They need different conditions at roosting places at different times of the year – basically hot in summer when the females are producing young and cold in winter when they are conserving energy by hibernating. It is rare for one roosting site to be suitable all year, so the bats move around to find new sites with just the right conditions. It is often hard to understand the links between members of a roost because they do not necessarily move as a unit but may break up to form smaller groups or even roost singly at times. Each species has its peculiarities, but generally in spring the adult females begin to gather together and in summer they produce their youngsters and wean them. At this time the males are roosting elsewhere away from all the fuss and performance of the nursery colonies and tend to be roosting in small numbers or singly. Some immature or non-breeding females

Looking up at a cluster of Daubenton's bats hanging from a tunnel roof.

may join the nursery roost. In early autumn the nursery colonies begin to move about and split into smaller groups. The summer holidays of the males are over, as they are now required for mating. By winter the bats have sought out hibernation sites where they may hibernate individually or in small groups with males, females and juveniles often segregated. In spring the females begin to gather into large groups again.

That is a very general summary. Close study of a single species will show up a number of variations in this pattern. It would be much easier to work out what happened if all the bats of a roost stayed together and all moved to a new site when necessary, but in practice some bats stay or may even move to a third, fourth or fifth site where they freely mingle with other bats of the same species from other sites. This adds enormous complications to the study of the social structures. It also shows that the bats found at one roost site may be just one part of a bigger 'colony' which lives in the area.

Pipistrelles have been studied for a number of years in many areas of Britain; but the more that is discovered about their groupings, the more

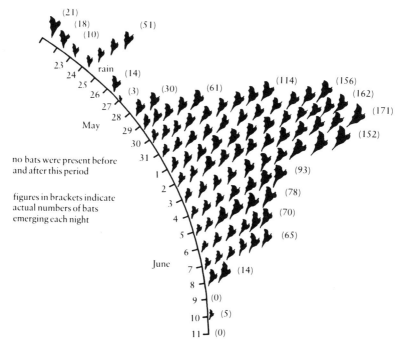

Nightly counts of Pipistrelles leaving a roost (Northants, 1984).

confusing the picture becomes. In my area they remain at a summer roosting site for anything between 1 and 31 (or more) days – an average of 12 days. They move at any time, even when they have babies: they just fly out with the youngster hanging on underneath.

This makes studying the roosting sites rather difficult and means moving fast or the bats will have gone before it is possible to assess the numbers present. At one house roost site the owner had noticed his bats for a week; when we arrived and waited outside for night-time emergence – not a single bat. The owner was adamant that they had been flying out on the previous night. A rather distraught lady then came running up the street to tell us that bats were pouring out of her house which was 200 yards away, and that she had never had bats before. The original roost-owner was rather annoyed by this and nearly asked for his bats back.

From repeated visits to roost sites over a number of years my bat group has noticed that Pipistrelles will use a site annually (well, almost annually) but not necessarily during the same part of the year, nor for the same length of time, nor by the same number of bats. At some sites we have noted the numbers using the roost place each day, and find that the numbers change almost nightly, generally with a rise then fall in numbers. This rather suggests that there is a 'rolling' population of Pipistrelles moving around the area, constantly changing sites. Sometimes in early autumn all the females and youngsters from many sites have a big get-together at one site which can cause a bit of anxiety for the house owner. The 55 kHz Pipistrelle species tends to be more settled and often will stay from May until September at the same site (although some do move around a bit). They also tend to have the larger gatherings – the biggest I encountered was almost 1,000! Pipistrelles do, however, seem a bit like the gypsies of the bat world and other species tend to be a little more predictable – in their use of roosting sites, at least; unfortunately few have yet been studied in any depth.

Bat roosts

Bats were originally cave- and tree-dwelling animals but many now find buildings just as suitable for their needs (which is fortunate since there are now far fewer trees available for bats – newly planted conifers contain few hollows and crevices when compared to an old oak). They may also use artificial caves in the form of mines and tunnels. Each bat species has special needs that must be fulfilled at each roosting site, such as the right temperature and humidity. The conditions change at each site throughout a season so the bats require a number of sites which they can visit and so select the best place to roost. All sites need to be well protected from disturbance and basically clean – no cobweb-infested attic would suffice for these very particular mammals. Bats will seek warm sites when they are rearing their naked young and cooler sites when they wish to be inactive and conserve energy such as when the weather is too bad for insects to fly.

Bats do not take bedding or nesting material into roost sites but rely entirely on the natural nooks and crannies to give them some shelter.

Tree roosts

Mature trees can provide a number of suitable roosting places – cracks and splits in willows, woodpecker holes in old oaks and beeches, crevices and holes in the soft, thick bark of Wellingtonias and hollow branches and loose bark on dead trees are amongst just some of the favoured sites. Some bats even roost on the outside of the tree but behind a dense covering of ivy.

The position of the tree is important. Daubenton's bats, for instance, use trees that are near, or overhanging, water; other species prefer trees in woodland but tend to use those situated along the edges of woodland or clearings. Parklands, with their well spaced and well matured trees, are also favoured.

Finding tree roosts is very difficult. Perhaps the easiest to locate in Britain are the tree roosts of Noctules. This large bat usually uses quite large holes and cracks – an old woodpecker hole in the tree trunk can be ideal. On a warm summer's day they may be heard chattering noisily from such holes (trunk calls!) and so can be located even from some distance. Unfortunately they do not always chatter and other species are often much quieter anyway so other methods of location have to be employed. I have spent many a happy day wandering around large tracts of woodlands with a 30-foot (10-metre) ladder, peering deep inside holes in trees in this search for bats (taking steps to find roosts).

A small mirror on a stick can aid the search especially in very small holes, and even a microphone on a long pole can be poked just inside a hole and used to eavesdrop on any bat-chat going on inside (ensure that your NCC licence covers you, of course; see Bats and the Law). Often such searches reveal nothing more than a few startled Starlings and maybe a disgruntled owl. Some tree roosts smell quite strongly of bats and have an entrance polished smooth by the passage of tiny bodies. Even when a roost is discovered then it is quite normal for it to be vacated after a few days because the bats use a number of similar sites in an area and like to move around. One bat group, after a great deal of hard work, managed to find a Noctule tree roost, but, on keeping a log of the numbers involved, the group soon twigged that some Noctules were not returning but spending days elsewhere. This led to them finding four tree roosts within half a mile of each other.

Noctules rely quite heavily on trees for roosting sites and rare species like Barbastelles and Bechstein's bats also seem to prefer woodland. Pipistrelles, however, commonly roost in buildings but there are always a few that stay in woodland and roost behind ivy or in crevices. Horseshoe bats are not into

trees at all and much prefer something a bit more substantial such as a cave or the roof of a derelict barn or house.

A major problem with tree roosts is that they are often lost when the trees are blown over in gales or when they are chopped down (trees with holes are uneconomic in commercially run woodland). The 1987 gales in the south of Britain actually helped Barbastelle bats. Some have now moved into the splits created as the top half of some trees were nearly snapped off by the wind. As if having their homes chopped down wasn't enough, the poor bats have to contend with bird problems too. Starlings like to take over old woodpecker holes and they will not live in harmony with any bats that might already be in residence. Usually the Starling is the victor, and there have been well documented cases where Starlings have evicted Noctules from such holes. In one case a young female Noctule was battered to death by a gang of angry Starlings and her corpse pushed out from the tree hole.

(opposite) *Noctules.*

House roosts

A large number of bats rely on houses to provide them with shelter. Different species seek different conditions and so the design and construction of a house can influence which bats use it. Bats roost in a number of places (see p. 59) but always require fairly clean, quiet and draught-free positions. It is often necessary to search for the signs of bats (see Bat Droppings) because many tuck themselves deep into crevices out of sight, but a few species do hang in exposed positions. Greater Horseshoe bats, for instance, will hang from attic beams in old houses and barns but require a large entrance hole such as a broken window or open hatchway which eliminates many houses. Long-eared bats are more widespread and also may be seen hanging from ridge beams in an attic. Although many are usually visible, they also sometimes roost between the underboarding or roofing felt and the tiles or slates of the roof and will also be found in the tunnel formed by the ridge tiles and ridge beams. They use this tunnel not only as a secluded roosting place but also as a main route between the inside of an attic and the exit hole, which may be under a ridge tile, under lead flashing around a chimney stack or under the eaves. Short of removing part of the roof, it is very difficult to count the exact number present in an attic but usually this species forms roosts of less than forty bats. Many regularly used sites are in large Victorian houses.

Natterer's and Whiskered bats prefer older houses too. They spend less time in exposed positions but are often tucked away behind the underboarding or above the ridge beams. Their exit holes can be anywhere in the roof and often some distance from the roosting place. As dusk approaches they can be heard slowly shuffling along the roof to reach the nearest exit. At one Whiskered Bat roost that I regularly visit they emerge from any of seven holes in the roof and this makes counting them very difficult; so it is necessary to surround the house with bat counters, all watching different exits. The numbers change seasonally but usually there are less than seventy at that site.

In the south of England Serotines may be found in houses, sometimes even in modern ones. They need a larger entrance than many other bats and this must limit which houses can be used. Once inside the roof, they move around until they find the most suitable roosting position which may be just under the eaves or perhaps on the chimney stack in the loft. Other species move their roosting positions in a similar way as the temperature and other factors change during the summer. Most bats roosting in houses form clusters so a group of ten Serotines will not take up much space even though they are large bats.

Pipistrelle emerging from gable end roost.

The Pipistrelle will, I suppose, always be the most successful house-roosting bat. Being very small, it can squeeze through narrow gaps that deter other species – slots less than ½ inch (10 mm.) wide have been used. In Northamptonshire we find 80% of our Pipistrelle roosts in houses built since 1960. A small gap between the soffit and the house wall (see illustration) gives access into a warm, clean roosting site inside the boxed-in eaves of a roof. If the conditions outside become too hot or too cold then they may move between the roofing felt and tiles, on top of the house wall or into the cavity of the wall. Equally suitable are the bat-sized gaps behind fascia boards or hanging tiles which are often found on modern house walls. A warped plank or slipped tile gives access to these ideal sites. Pipistrelles form much larger roosts than other species at some times of the year and, being small bats, a large number can squeeze into a very small area. I've watched them emerging from the top three rows of hanging tiles above a garage door and, with the help of a team of counters, counted 717 fly out in 40 minutes. Such large roosts are unusual; 200–300 regularly occur but 50–150 is the usual number. They move roosts regularly and also split up into smaller groups so even the smaller roost sites are used for only short periods of time. The roost owner with the 717 bats was more than happy with the final count and we toasted their success in whisky after the last few had emerged. Pipistrelles, like many bats, prefer to roost high up, so often choose a gable end wall and roost as close to the top as possible. The habit of Pipistrelles roosting on the outside of the house rather than being inside the attic is well worth pointing out to the roost-owner if he is a little worried about the new lodgers – not that they cause any damage anyway.

Whiskered Bat roost in house loft.

Large cellars provide good sites for some species. Access must be possible through open windows or through an open outside door and the cellar must be little used by people. Horseshoe bats find such places extremely attractive. Open porches and any covered area next to a house may be used by bats as a temporary roost site during the night. In fact there is a large number of possible places for bats to roost in any house; houses have become of major importance to the bat population.

Occasionally, particularly in autumn, bats are found inside the living accommodation of a house. Usually only a single bat has been so brave and it will have entered by accident through an open window – possibly seeking a hibernation site. In some old country mansions bats fly regularly along the corridors acting as if they owned the place. In one such Hall I visited the bats were sneaking in from their roosting site in a stone wall and meandering around the house at tiara-height, occasionally frightening the odd titled lady staying there as a guest. The bats were entering through one of twenty bathrooms up in the servants' quarters. This was rather an exceptional case and usually any bat inside a house is desperately seeking a way out. If a window is left open then they will often find this escape route but if a bat lands on a wall, then carefully cover it in a soft cloth, pick it up and release it gently

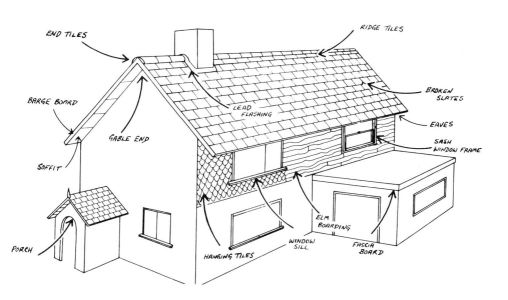

Access and roosting places.

outside (preferably after dark). Indoors it is rather difficult to find them if the exact resting place is not pinpointed. At one site I visited the lady of the house had ensured that no one disturbed the bat that she had seen in her living room by sealing up the door with sticky tape. I managed to unstick my way in and searched for 15 minutes in vain. Eventually I found a Pipistrelle tucked into one of the pleats on the curtains which was quite amazing because I had carefully drawn the curtains back and forth a number of times in my search – it must have been getting quite giddy. Bats can get into any room because they can creep under closed doors, but they are frequently found in bathrooms, possibly because the gaps around the water pipes may provide a way in from the attic. Bedrooms are also often visited mainly because many people sleep with the window open.

As usual there are always a few extroverts that turn up in the most unusual places. I've come across odd bats under floorboards, in a pan of a toilet (looking rather flushed), in an electric light switch fitting in a house under construction and even in a bath tap which had to be dismantled to remove the bat.

House conversion

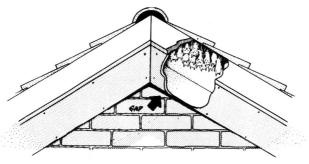

Gable end of a house.

If you want to encourage bats to roost in your house, here are some suggestions that will not affect the structure of your house.

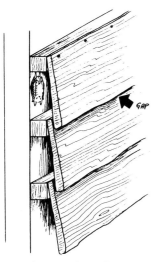

Overlapping boards.

Roofs: *access slots need to be made under the eaves at a gable end and near to the highest point. Also provide an entrance under ridge tiles by chipping out some of the cement and/or by lifting the lead flashing near the chimney.*
Inside ensure that there is access by providing a gap in the roofing felt near the entry holes. Brush away any dust and cobwebs from the rafters and nail a few panels of fibre board onto the rafters just below the ridge to provide a sheltered area.

Outside walls: *attach ½ inch (3 cm.) battens to the upper part of a gable end wall (south or west side) and nail on horizontal overlapping boards or hanging tiles, remembering to leave entrance holes to the gap behind.*

Church roosts

Bats have long been associated with churches, which certainly provide some excellent roosting places – real sanctuaries for bats. With one in almost every village in Britain, churches play an important role. Although cooler than house roosts, they are quieter for most of the week but do tend to become a bit noisy on Sundays.

Many traditional types of church buildings have been added to or repaired over the centuries and this gives rise to a number of suitable crevices for roosting bats. Most are in the church roof with favourite sites being between the chancel and nave, nave and tower, above the altar and in the aisle roof. Bats squeeze between the roof timbers and the church walls, and find plenty of roosting space between underboarding and the lead or tile roof covering. Some bats can even be found roosting behind notice boards and wooden hangings on the walls.

Gaining access to these sites inside a church can test a bat's ingenuity. Some enter easily enough under the eaves of the roof or through gaps or holes in the lead flashing on the roof; these may only lead to the roof, not to the church itself, and many a bat lives happily in such a place without setting a wing inside the church at all. Some good roosting places, however, are only accessible from inside the church and so entry may be gained through a broken window or, more commonly, over the church door. These old wooden doors are usually very heavy and sink on their hinges, leaving a bat-sized crack at the top which Pipistrelles, for instance, love to squeeze through. In one church I know a bat regularly squeezed over the top of the closed porch door, flew through the porch, squeezed over the main church door, then flew up inside the church to a roof crevice which it entered with a bit more squeezing, doubtless pretty thin by this time.

The porches, especially the roofs, also make good roosting sites. One summer my bat group looked at all 285 church porches in Northamptonshire and found that almost a third were used by bats. Although Pipistrelles were the most regularly found species there were also Natterer's, Long-eared and even Daubentons' bats at some sites. Other species can be found around churches, of course, although some, such as Serotines and Noctules, require bigger crevices and more roosting space.

Although belfries have been famed for bats, they are not the best places to find them. If the bells are rung regularly then the disturbance is great for any dozing bat – they don't find the sound of bells ap-pealing! The louvres make the towers draughty places and often birds gain entry which may disturb any bats (see p. 55). Some belfries are quieter, but I rarely find any sign of bats in them. Bats outside often fly close by the tower at night, sometimes circling it and this may have been the reason for its unwarranted fame as a bat roost.

Bats have an unfortunate and unexplained habit of flying round and round inside big, open buildings at night; they demonstrate this often in churches. Little feeding seems to be taking place and the reasons for this odd behaviour are not clear. It is unfortunate, because it causes an even spread of bat droppings in all corners of the church which can annoy the cleaners and the vicar. Covering over sensitive areas with cloths alleviates the problem. Brasses and marble on the floor should be protected anyway, or thousands of human feet will wear away the surface making the droppings problem insignificant. If small numbers of bats are present then the 'church mouse' always gets the blame.

Churches can be used in all seasons if the conditions are right. The stone walls can give conditions very similar to those in caves, so some bats will hibernate there. They are also used at night; Long-eared bats, for instance, may often be seen hanging up on the roof beams at night; discarded moth wings, the remnants of a bat feast, will form a small pile below.

Bats in churches are often fun. I have been sent some very detailed notes concerning bats that were carefully observed during church services. At one evening service the vicar was commemorating the Battle of Britain and as he spoke of the exploits of the RAF a Pipistrelle repeatedly swooped low over the pulpit causing the vicar to duck; the congregation found it most amusing. In one small village the parishioners are so proud of their Natterer's bats that they suggested fixing a mirror under the roosting place so that the choir could watch the bats during the services. I reminded them that the poor bats would also be able to see in the mirror and might be frightened at the sight of a dozen people grinning up at them. On reflection they dropped the mirror idea.

One wonderfully large Natterer's roost in a porch was of national importance so we monitored it regularly. This involved catching a few at dusk with a net across the entrance to see the age and sex of the bats. Everyone had been told of our study, but clerics' memories are sometimes short and the local vicar came breezing up the church path with a hearty wave and 'Good evening, my children' as he walked straight into the net. It took some time to extricate him, the dog collar getting particularly entangled.

Brown Long-eared Bat.

Cave roosts

Bats will use not just caves but any cave-like structures – tunnels, mines, grottoes, ice-houses, cellars, ruined castles, underground fortifications and similar. The temperature of these places is buffered from outside so can remain cold. These are much sought after in winter for hibernation, although bats may use them in summer for night-roosting. Individual bats may use the same crevice deep inside a pitch-black cave system every winter, showing that they have an excellent memory based on the sound picture built up with echo-location. Humidity is vital in winter and needs to be high. The best sites will also give a variety of different low temperatures so different species can all benefit. Subtle changes in temperature or humidity will wake up the bats and can cause them to move – even standing under a bat will cause the temperature to rise enough for arousal. In warmer countries than Britain bats regularly use warm caves for day-roosting, often chosen in preference to buildings. Humans, however, are also attracted to underground sites both in summer and winter, and their unintentional disturbance can drive the bats out so the best sites for bats have to be protected.

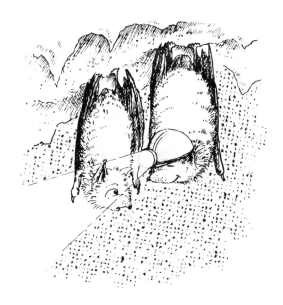

The town bat

Although bats are often associated with villages, woodlands and the countryside there is many a bat in the town. Plenty of good accommodation and food is to be had if they know where to look. Housing is more diverse than in villages so the choice of roost site is greater for those bats that live in buildings – maybe a centrally heated semi-detached house on the edge of town or a nice warm office block only a few seconds' flight from the town centre. Some bats have even been reported using crevices on tower blocks (flat bats?).

Towns don't offer the diversity of insects that the countryside provides, but they have sufficient places where a reasonable number can be found. Many towns, for instance, have rivers running close by, which usually have plenty of insects. The bright city lights are an attraction to insects, which congregate around stadium floodlights, some street lights and airport lamps, and bats soon come along to feed. Town parks provide quite a variety of insect life: some have small lakes and I have found Daubenton's Bat, a species which feeds principally on aquatic insects, on such a pool only a mile from a town centre. Pipistrelles can be found right in the town centre although their main feeding areas may be further afield. Old Victorian factories and associated terraced rows of houses may be home to small numbers of Long-eared bats.

One summer I surveyed the town of Northampton at night using a bat detector to locate flying bats and was pleasantly surprised at the numbers in the area, although they were concentrated in a number of large parks, churchyards and along the River Nene. Using a detector in such an area is not easy because it picks up a number of other noises apart from bats – the squeaky wheels of a bicycle, the brakes of a bus or even people walking on gravel. All of these have to be carefully distinguished from bat calls. In one park I picked up a most unusual noise, pointed my spotlight in the direction of the sound and illuminated a courting couple passionately kissing; I had to beat a hasty retreat with angry threats ringing in my ears. Another odd 'chonk' noise I detected was far more bat-like but was coming from under a bush – hardly the place to find a flying bat! Closer investigation proved this to be coming from a grumpy old hedgehog. But it was good to see bats deep inside our concrete jungles; wherever you live in Britain there is always the chance to do some batting.

Bat droppings

They may only be waste to a bat but they are bread and butter to the bat worker as they give vital clues as to the presence of bats, their eating habits (see Bat Grub) and even to the identification of species. Although at first glance they look similar to mouse droppings, the connoisseur can easily tell them apart – they crumble to a fine powder of insect fragments when rubbed between finger and thumb whereas fresh mice droppings are slimy and you soon wish you hadn't embarked on the test. Old mice droppings are rock hard, whereas old bat droppings tend to turn to powder. Rat poison and mouse traps are commonly encountered in bat roosts showing that many of their hosts are confused too. One of 'my' roost owners, whose front step was covered in droppings, used to leave a mouse trap on the doorstep amongst her empty milk bottles at night before she realized that the droppings were from a roost high up under the eaves above the front door. Her milkman complained bitterly one morning when he discovered the trap as he fumbled for the order note in the early morning light – eaves dropping wasn't necessary to hear his remarks.

Another way to distinguish bat from mouse droppings is to look at the location – bat droppings are commonly found on the side of the wall beneath the roost entrance and it would take a very determined mouse with pitons to reach such a site and then deposit its droppings.

Bats vary in size, in their diets and in the degree to which they grind up their food, and their droppings reflect these differences in variations of size, shape and texture; this provides a guide as to the identity of the bat involved. Different species roost in different places and in different ways within roosts, so the position of the accumulations of droppings can also be used in identification. Long-eared Bat droppings, for instance, are found in long lines under the ridge beam of an attic roost, whereas Pipistrelles do not hang from the ridge beams in such an exposed manner so their droppings are not deposited in this way.

The droppings will be concentrated around and under the roost entrance so can be used to pinpoint the roosting place. The sudden appearance of droppings at a known roost site will tell you that bats have returned; they are a useful guide to the comings and goings of the bats. In big buildings such as churches or factories the floors will be regularly swept, so many of the signs of the presence of bats will be lost, but high ledges or the walls themselves will still have a number of these tell-tale signs since the bats fly around extensively in such buildings at night.

Bat droppings are not at all offensive: they consist almost entirely of indigestible fragments of insects, and are no health hazard. One lady roost-owner was unconvinced when I told her this whilst crumbling up a few droppings in my fingers. She then offered me a biscuit and was only persuaded when I had eaten it and licked my fingers. In normal dry conditions they have only a faint aroma. (At least, faint to us, but it has been suggested that odour is very important to bats. Some artificial roosting places have been ignored by these temperamental animals until a quantity of droppings was added to give the right atmosphere.)

Droppings are not appreciated by everyone and large roosts can at times leave quite a mess in houses and churches and cause alarm to some people. Once initial fears about health problems have been dispelled then the only problem is cleaning up the mess. The easiest solution is to catch the droppings with covers and shake them periodically. In attics most droppings fall beneath the ridge beam, so any stored belongings are better stacked on either side of this area and, if necessary, covered in cloths. The erection of false ceilings or partitions in attics limits the problem quite satisfactorily but does need NCC approval (see p. 107). Roosts on the outside of a building cause less of a problem unless droppings land on window ledges or doorsteps. A narrow ledge fixed a few feet beneath the roost entrance or just above a window will protect all below from the black rain. The problem in churches is more difficult, but covering up sensitive areas with plastic sheets or cloths is the simplest and cheapest solution. Pew seat cushions should be turned over after use. In all sites the droppings are only present for part of the year – during the long winter months there will be no sign of bats. Drastic action rarely seems worthwhile with such a temporary problem.

In some countries the droppings build up beneath large roosts to such an extent that they can be collected and sold as fertilizer. In Britain the roosts are much smaller but it may be possible to collect enough to nourish a small window-box.

Dropping collections

The well equipped bat enthusiast always walks around with a labelled collection of droppings from different bat species (preferably in a different pocket from his snuff). Direct comparisons can then be made with any droppings found. This work is best carried out in daytime as the droppings are not always easy to find. The length and shape of the black or brown droppings are important and so is the composition – the fragments may be very fine or coarse. Also note the location of the droppings and the type of building being used. A collection of droppings from a species is easier to use than single droppings and with practice it is possible to obtain a good idea of the species of bat involved and sometimes even positively identify it by its droppings.

A few helpful pointers are listed opposite for droppings most often encountered.

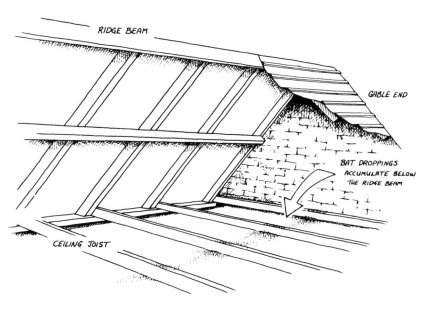

Typical site of droppings in loft.

SPECIES	TYPICAL LOCATION	COMPOSITION	DESCRIPTION
Whiskered	Attics, churches	M	Almost as small as Pipistrelle. In attics often under the ridge beams in lines but with marked clusters.
Natterer's	Churches, attics	C	Coarse, granular and fat. Often in 3 parts.
Daubenton's	Tunnels, stone structures, churches	M/F	Long, thin.
Serotine	Attics, churches	C	Pellet or capsule shaped, round ended. Brown or black. Fat.
Noctule	Trees. Rare in houses, cellars and churches	C	Fat. Blunt.
Pipistrelle	Outside walls of houses, churches	F	Very fine. Thin. Small. Often tapered at one end.
Brown Long-eared	Attics, churches	M	Shiny 'varnished' surface; most black, some brown. Often 2 or 3 parts. Moth wings often nearby.

Key to composition column: M = medium, C = coarse and F = fine

This list is simplified. Experience is essential. Droppings vary greatly during the year when insects become scarce or when new insects take to the wing.

Serotine   Natterer's   Pipistrelle

Roost emergence

One of the more spectacular sights during summer is bats coming out of their roost sites at dusk – known as 'emergence'. Just before sunset the bats start to become active and within the roost there are movements and scratchings, stretching and yawnings, and usually lots of chattering. Soon after sunset they begin to emerge and fly off to feeding areas. The emergence is not haphazard but seems to follow set patterns.

Emergence times

Are closely linked to the time of sunset, which can easily be shown if you record the times of first-emerging bats at a number of sites throughout the summer (see opposite). The chart also shows that different species begin to emerge at different times, a fact that is probably related to individual feeding preferences. Many roosts are situated deep inside buildings or tunnels and little light penetrates, yet the bats always seem to know when dusk is falling and that it is time to feed. At one tunnel I visit no light penetrates (it is like looking for a black bat in a coal cellar) but when my luminous watch tells me that dusk has fallen outside the resident bats begin to wake up and depart. This remarkable ability is caused by a sort of internal clock – known as 'circadian' activity rhythm. A similar system operates in humans and is most noticeable when we travel long distances by jet. If we fly to the United States, for instance, the airport clocks tell us that it is the middle of the afternoon, yet our body clock tells us that it is time to sleep and it really should be night-time just as it is back in Europe. Within a few days our 'clock' has adjusted to the new conditions and this 'jet-lag' is no longer a problem. In a similar way bats can adjust their internal timing systems to cope with the differing lengths of daylight in summer; but, like our own circadian rhythm, it probably takes a few days to change and this will buffer the bat against any short-term change in weather conditions.

Extreme weather conditions such as strong winds, low temperatures or rain delay bats in coming out. But they are not absolutely rigorous time keepers even when weather conditions are normal. Why not? A number of studies have looked at temperature, wind speed and direction, light intensity and moonlight to see if these cause the variations, but few, if any, links have been found. The outside light intensity, for instance, has always been thought to affect emergence time. If this was the only factor then bats would be expected to emerge earlier from shaded east or north facing roosts than from the roosts facing the brighter western sky. This does not appear to be the case,

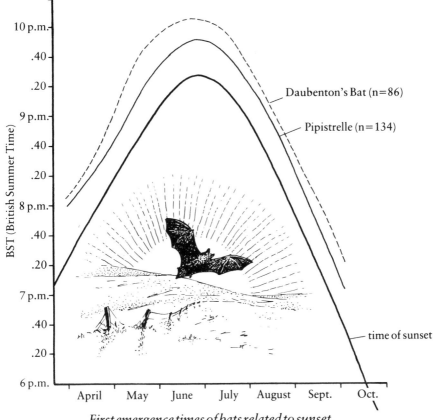

First emergence times of bats related to sunset.

nor do bats always emerge earlier on overcast nights. Bats' general independence of outside conditions was highlighted for me one evening when we were studying three Pipistrelle roosts which were in neighbouring buildings. Emergence time at one house was 15 minutes before that of the other two although the same environmental conditions applied to all three sites. We do not know the reason for variations, but some answers may be found when more information about the conditions within a roosting place has been collected and the exact function of each site has been discovered.

As a guide for the bat watcher the times of first emergence of some species widespread over much of Britain are given in the table overleaf. These were all recorded in Northamptonshire and geographical variations are always possible.

	Ave. emergence time after sunset (mins)	Extremes (mins)	No. of roosts in sample
Whiskered Bat	30	0–45	5
Natterer's Bat	38	25–60	19
Daubenton's Bat	45	11–77	86
Noctule	30	13–55	30
Pipistrelle	20–25	7–55	134

Emergence patterns

Bats do not all emerge together and there seem to be patterns which become more obvious if the nightly rate of emergence is measured. Just stand outside the roost site and count how many fly out every minute. Times when the largest numbers emerge soon become apparent (see below); usually, there are up to three peaks when most numbers come out, in the case of the Pipistrelle for instance. In summer the adult females come out first, then youngsters big

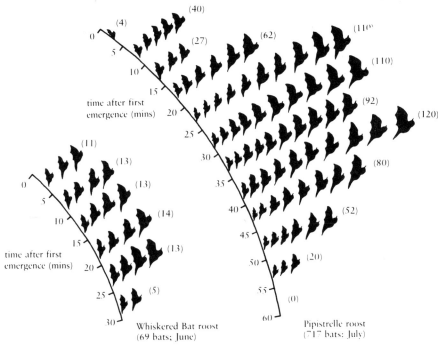

Patterns of emergence from roosts (figures in brackets indicate actual numbers of bats emerging within a five-minute period).

enough to fly follow in a second burst of activity. As with most bat work it is not as straightforward as it first seems: sometimes there is only one burst of activity, consisting of bats of both age groups. Further study is obviously necessary to discover more about these fascinating emergence peaks and amateur studies can be profitably carried out in this area (see Project section).

After the first bat has left the roost there is often a short delay before the rest follow. They seem to come out in groups rather than in a steady stream, with often 4 or 5 shooting out together. At some roosts of Pipistrelles it

appears that what happens is that a few sit at the entrance to the roost, then more press up from behind and so 'urge' them out. The rates at which they all come out have been studied for few species: Pipistrelles all seem to have emerged after 45–60 minutes, although Long-eared and Whiskered bats emerge more quickly. One would imagine that a very large number of bats would take longer to emerge but, for Pipistrelles anyway, they just come out more quickly and still have all left within an hour after the first appeared.

Although most bats leave their roosts to forage at dusk there always seem to be a few that remain inside. The numbers are difficult to ascertain because many roosting sites are not accessible, but probably very few are involved.

Once, however, whilst trying to watch the emergence of a colony of Daubenton's bats from inside a very wet and uncomfortable tunnel I noted that they woke up at dusk, then promptly fell asleep again and remained there all night – very frustrating.

Emergence watching can give us important information about the bats. I have noticed that at some Pipistrelle roosts emerging female numbers are stable each night, then when the youngsters start flying out the numbers do not increase. This indicates that their mothers have already deserted the roost, possibly as an encouragement for the juniors to start flying and fending for themselves. I assume that the other adults emerging have young inside too small to fly.

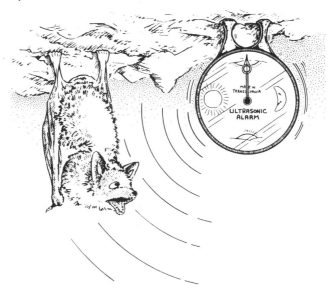

Bats on their travels

Bats have three main reasons for moving from one area to another – food, shelter and sex.

Food

Food is not always conveniently flying around just outside the roost site, and even if it were then the first emerging bats would snaffle everything before the last in line had even left the roost place. Individuals have favourite feeding places which they visit in turn throughout the night. These sites, which they may share with other bats, may contain one particular type of insect for the short period of its life, so the bats need a number of different sites to visit to cope with seasonal changes in insects. The few British bat species that have been studied seem to range well over a mile (1½ km) from their roosting site in search of food, with bigger species going much further. Noctules have been recorded flying over 6 miles (10 km) to feed, and have been recorded visiting rubbish tips when crickets are emerging. (The Noctule is a cricket bat.) Long-eared bats usually forage within ½ km of the roost, but may travel about 2 miles (nearly 3 km) from the roost.

When they have arrived at feeding areas bats fly backwards and forwards, often along regular flight paths and are likely, therefore, to fly many tens of miles within the limited area. They do not fly continuously all night, but find a night-time roost site and put their feet up (quite literally) for a while. Tracking bats as they feed at night is not easy: sophisticated techniques such as radio-tracking help a lot, but radios are very expensive (see p. 93).

My local bat group began to study the feeding ranges of Daubenton's bats along canals and could not afford radio transmitters, so initially we ran flat out along the towpaths to try to keep up with the bats as they skimmed along the surface of the canal. Unfortunately they fly at about 15 m.p.h. (25 k.p.h.) which is a little above my running speed, so they soon pulled ahead and disappeared into the distance. Hurdling barge mooring ropes in the dark was an added problem, and the water voles didn't help by tunnelling up into the towpath to create man-traps. Recently we have adopted the more sophisticated technique of setting out a chain of bat workers along the canal with walkie-talkie radios so that the progress of the bats can be monitored. In this way we have learnt that Daubenton's bats regularly travel 1¼ miles (2 kilometres) from the roost site, sometimes 3 miles (5 kilometres) and apparently even 6 miles (10 kilometres) occasionally – not bad for a mammal only a couple of inches long.

Shelter

Shelter for bats is vital, but it must also be the correct site for particular conditions – and lots of roost-swapping takes place (see p. 52). During summer these movements tend to be within a small area, most sites being less than ½ mile (1 kilometre) apart. When it is time to search out hibernation sites, then bats may have to travel a little further. The Greater Horseshoe Bat, the most studied bat in Britain, occasionally will move up to 40 miles (64 kilometres) and will often move 6 miles (10 kilometres) from one hibernation site to another. On the Continent bats arrive at favourite hibernation sites from greater distances, often more than 100 miles (160 kilometres) or more away.

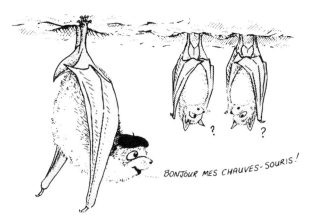

BONJOUR MES CHAUVES-SOURIS!

Some bat species in the world undergo migrations to avoid adverse weather conditions. Hoary bats in the USA, for example, move south below latitude 37°N in winter and then migrate back into Canada and Alaska in summer. In Europe real migrations have been difficult to prove but Pipistrelles and Noctules can both move long distances from the extreme north of their range southwards with records of both species travelling well over 500 miles (800 kilometres). Hints of migrations of bats occur periodically when bats are found in odd places or out of their normal range – a Parti-coloured Bat on an oil rig 170 miles (270 kilometres) off the north-east coast of Britain in 1965; a Brown Long-eared Bat on a lightship 50 miles (80 kilometres) off the Norfolk coast, and isolated records of Noctules in the Orkneys are just a few examples. Doubtless there are other migrant bats that pass unrecorded as they will not be separable from the native bats of the same species in the area. When studies of bird migrations at night were conducted using radar, some of the unidentified 'blips' were assumed to be bats but unfortunately no further work has been carried out.

Sex

In the autumn females from the summer nursery colonies and males come together for mating. Quite how they meet is unclear, but some roosting sites are visited by both sexes in autumn – sort of lonelyhearts clubs. In the case of the Noctule, the females go looking for a male and visit him in his tree roost where he sets up a type of stud farm for bats. Pipistrelles and other species are also believed to act in this way. Females are unlikely to travel far to meet the male and seem to stick within the area of the summer roosts or the winter hibernating places.

Homing

Although bats move about during summer or between summer and winter sites, individuals will often be found using the same sites each year, and sometimes even the same crevice year after year. This indicates that they have good memories. Experiments have been carried out by releasing bats at different distances from their roosting places and it has been clearly shown that they soon find their way back over a couple of miles. Greater distances result in fewer returning, but, given the fact that bats have several roosting sites, it would be normal for a displaced bat to seek shelter in the nearest roost that it recognized, not necessarily returning to the roost it was taken from.

Their navigation system is hard to understand: their echo-location is not really suitable for building up a picture of the countryside as it has quite a short range, but their eyes are especially adapted to low light levels, so eyesight seems more suitable. Perhaps a combination of these two and other senses is utilized.

Before the 1981 Wildlife and Countryside Act gave protection to all bats one roost-owner in my area appeased his nagging mother-in-law by getting rid of a Pipistrelle roost in his eaves simply by putting them in a sack and carting them to a wood about a mile away before releasing them. On returning home he found that the bats had beaten him to it and were all happily back in the roost chattering about their nice little ride in the country. He gave up any further attempts and said it was mother-in-law's turn next if there were any more complaints.

Long-distance migrations must be more than just memory: it has been suggested that use of the Earth's magnetic field may play a part, as with bird migrations, but it is a very complex topic and will require far more research before we are likely to understand how bats manage to navigate.

The Homing Bat, Boomerangus domesticus.

Bat conservation

To ensure that bats continue to grace our skies at night means conservation, not just of the bats, but of their hibernacula, roosting sites and food supplies.

Bat protection

Fortunately in Britain people have no interest in bats as food items, bat pelts have no commercial value and bats offer no sporting interest. They are still killed, however, through the mistaken belief that they are a health hazard or cause damage to buildings, through intolerance by people in living in close proximity with them and through wanton vandalism. Legislation (see Bats and the Law) has made it illegal to kill bats, but to prevent such unnecessary deaths people need to be educated. A blossoming interest in bats has helped to make the plights of many species more widely known. Correcting the image of the British bat from a thing of Draculean terror to a small, cuddly and sensitive creature in urgent need of help and understanding is also helping to gain sympathetic responses from the general public.

Hibernacula protection

Disturbing hibernating bats causes them to become active and use up some of their limited fat reserves. Hibernacula, therefore, need to be places that are free from disturbance. Many sites are caves and mines and such holes in the ground hold a special fascination for people: caving and potholing have become very popular pastimes. The echoing noises, the lights and the change in temperature caused by people entering a cave will rouse any hibernating bats. One solution has been to fix barriers across the entrances of the more important hibernation caves and mines. These consist of horizontal bars which are too close to allow a person to squeeze between but wide enough to allow bats to enter. More solid barriers may alter the fine balance of air currents which keep the caves at a specific humidity and temperature level. Disused mines are dangerous places and many have been sealed up to prevent injury especially to children. This has resulted in the loss of hibernacula. More interest in bats in recent times has ensured that now they are closed with grilles so that they may still be used by bats, this being in accordance with recent laws which make it an offence to obstruct the entrances to hibernacula. Hibernation places are so sensitive that even experienced bat workers do not visit them regularly for fear of disturbing the bats – a visit once or twice each winter is enough and enables the researcher to count the species and numbers present.

Grilled cave entrance.

Summer roost protection

Houses are commonly used in summer as roost sites and give excellent protection if the roost owner is tolerant but could be dangerous if he or she is anti-bat. Initially many roost-owners are a little apprehensive when their little guests first move in, but once they have been told of the lives and problems of bats in the modern world they usually become part of the bat protection squad. Many hundreds of householders are involved in looking after bats and their efforts are helping to slow the decline in bat populations (see p. 89). Concern over the falling numbers of bats helped to give them legal protection. Fortunately, the great British public are mostly animal lovers at heart and their very own roost of bats is something well worth boasting about to the neighbours. We enjoy birds living in our gardens; why not bats too?

Poisoning is the worst problem affecting bats in buildings. Many roofs are treated to eradicate woodworm and death-watch beetle and the poisons kill bats too. This is a large and very serious problem as many tens of thousands of roofs are treated annually. Some of the poisons used are so powerful that even pets have died. Any bat coming into contact with freshly treated wood will be dead within a day or two. The poisons are long-lasting and any bat moving into such a roof even years after the treatment is likely to be affected. Preparations containing lindane, for example, are very harmful and such 'over-kill' seems unnecessary, and who knows what effects they may be having on us too. Other, more selective poisons are now available containing permethrin which still kills the wood-boring pests but has little effect on bats or other mammals. If bats are present in a roof then no form of timber treatment can be carried out until the advice of the NCC has been sought: they can suggest the most suitable chemical to use and also the best time to apply it.

The full effects of poisons such as lindane are unknown. Small doses kill bats: traces may not kill, yet still have some effect – a general weakness will shorten their lives and decrease their reproducing capacity. The best conservation measure is to use milder treatments such as permethrin and avoid using any 'stronger' poisons.

Summer roosts may be in tree holes or crevices. Old and dying trees have a number of possible roosting places so should be left standing and not cut down to 'tidy up' or because they have no commercial value. Ivy coverings are a bonus so killing of the ivy should be avoided. Where such trees have been lost then bat roosting boxes (see p. 87) should be erected to redress the situation. Conserving dead trees seems a contradiction but they are vital for some bats.

Food supply protection

There has been a general decline in the number of insects in Britain due in part to the widespread use of insecticides on farmlands, in woodlands and in gardens. Insects can still fly when they have small amounts of poison in them but the poison is passed on to any predator. DDT was widely used after the late 1940s and aldrin, dieldrin and heptachlor were used after 1955. The latter caused dramatic declines in the numbers of raptors such as the Sparrowhawk. The decline was due in part to the thinning of their eggshells which then broke in the nest. What effect these poisons are having on bats is unknown, but bats similarly accumulate the poisons and are unusually sensitive to them. Although there is not the problem of eggshell thinning, it is likely that the poisons affect reproduction.

Changing agricultural practice also affects numbers of insects. Pressure on the farming community to produce more food as cheaply and efficiently as possible has led to huge alterations to the agricultural landscape. The use of machinery to sow and harvest crops is good for efficiency but only in larger fields of one crop. Hedgerows have, therefore, been removed and the diversity of farm crops has been lost, resulting in decreases in both numbers and varieties of insects. Many insects must complete their life cycle in grassland, often reaching the adult stage when the grasses are ripe. Hayfields are havens for insects (unless sprayed with poisons) but now silage is being more widely used for cattle feeding. Silage involves cutting the grass before it has matured and, in the process, killing numerous insects whilst they are still larvae or pupae, and therefore not available to the bats. Many beetles such as the cockchafer rely on unimproved meadowland for their life cycle, and silage-making seems to be affecting the numbers of these valuable insects – valuable that is to bats such as the rare Greater Horseshoe (shown opposite) which shows a preference for them.

Woodlands have also changed dramatically. The insect-rich deciduous woods at the turn of the century have been replaced in many areas by more 'economic' conifer plantations. Conifers have fewer associated insects both within the trees and in the limited flora beneath.

Insects depend upon different types of plants for their life cycles. Where the vegetation is varied then so is the insect life. Variety is important whether it is trees in a wood, crops grown on a farm or even plants and shrubs grown in a garden. And without a good supply of healthy insects our bats will suffer greater declines. The latest possible threat comes from genetically modified plant material – farmers' crops and trees. Any with a resistance to insect depredations are likely to affect the numbers of those insects and so affect availability of bat food. Further, less obvious links, will no doubt show themselves when they come into full production.

All forms of bat conservation rely on the good sense and good will of the public. Most will be happy to help if they know how, and so education is very important. Anyone coming into contact with bats should be aware of the special and delicate position that these creatures have in the world.

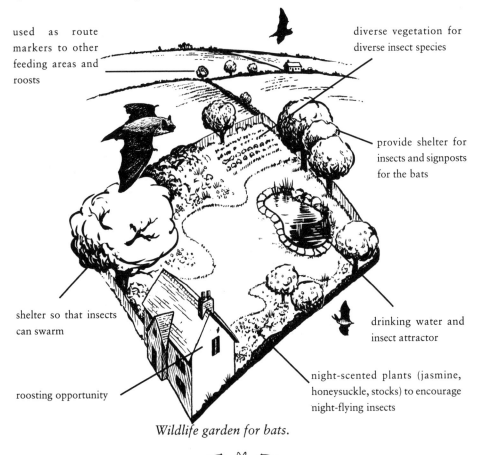

used as route markers to other feeding areas and roosts

diverse vegetation for diverse insect species

provide shelter for insects and signposts for the bats

shelter so that insects can swarm

drinking water and insect attractor

roosting opportunity

night-scented plants (jasmine, honeysuckle, stocks) to encourage night-flying insects

Wildlife garden for bats.

Bat boxes

Artificial roosting boxes for bats have been in use for many decades. Originally they were put up in areas of woodland or marshland to encourage bats to move in and keep down the numerous insect pests. Dr Campbell's efforts in mosquito-infested areas of Texas, USA, in 1911 were grandiose – huge wooden towers on stilts. He had some success but similar towers put up in Europe were shunned by bats. They seem to prefer smaller boxes, which are now widely used to conserve bats by providing roosting places in areas devoid of alternative sites. Bat roosting boxes are similar to wooden bird nest boxes but instead of an entrance hole in the front there is a narrow slot underneath. Such entrances seem favoured by bats and also exclude most birds, although tits and Treecreepers do still get in at times. The wood must be unplaned, untreated and at least ¾ inch (2 cm.) thick – the rough surface provides footholds for the bats; any wood treatment has an unpleasant smell that is not appreciated by bats and the thick wood gives plenty of protection from changes in temperature outside. The life of these untreated boxes can be lengthened by covering the tops in heavy-duty polythene or with pieces of

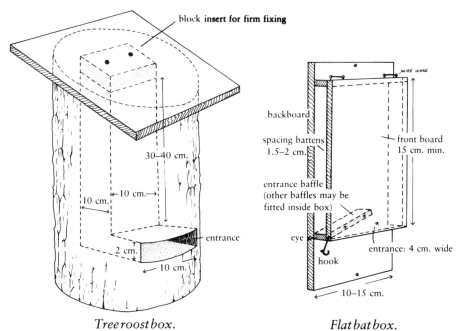

Tree roost box.

Flat bat box.

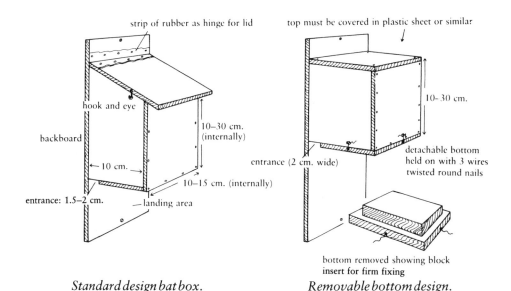

strip of rubber as hinge for lid

top must be covered in plastic sheet or similar

hook and eye

backboard

10–30 cm.
(internally)

10–30 cm.

entrance (2 cm. wide)

detachable bottom
held on with 3 wires
twisted round nails

← 10 cm.

10–15 cm. (internally)

entrance: 1.5–2 cm.

landing area

bottom removed showing block
insert for firm fixing

Standard design bat box.

Removable bottom design.

roofing felt. The slot size is most important and must not be too wide. The exact size of the box is not critical; suggested sizes are given although the width of the available wood usually governs the size.

The success of the boxes as bat roosts depends less upon the design than on the location. They are most successful when placed in coniferous woodland where few alternative roosting places exist. The boxes should be positioned so that they are in the warmth of the sun for part of the day, so the edge of the woodland and facing south or west is best. The boxes should be firmly fixed as high as possible on a sturdy main trunk and the entrance should be free from any obstructions such as branches. Bats often move between different roost places so three boxes attached to the same tree and facing in different directions will enable the bats to select the best conditions. Clustering the boxes in one area of woodland can also improve the chances of them being used. Such boxes may be used at any time of the year but, as with other types of roost sites, bats may stay for only short periods. Sometimes up to forty bats may use the box. A variety of species may be involved, such as Long-eared Bat, Noctule or Leisler's, but compared to bird boxes the success rate is low; it may be several years before they are used. Although greatest success is achieved with large projects involving hundreds of boxes in woodland it is possible that a few boxes in a garden may be used, particularly if nearby roosting places have been recently lost. Bat droppings in the bottom of the box will indicate usage.

Population levels

An assessment of the size of the population of bats in Britain is a most important part of bat conservation. It indicates those species that are declining in number and also serves as a guide to the effectiveness of various methods used to conserve bats. Unfortunately it is very difficult to count bats: they roost in well hidden and inaccessible places, often move roosting places, do not remain in one group but split up into smaller roosts which are even more difficult to find, and they can be very sensitive to any disturbance in a roost site and bolt for cover as soon as the bat counter arrives – all this as well as the fact that one is trying to count dark bats in dark places causes endless problems. Counts at some very large, popular roosting or hibernating places at least give an indication of changes in numbers. In the Netherlands the huge expanse of the St Pietersberg mines in South Limburg is used in winter by over 3,000 bats, many of which come from a wide surrounding area. Annual counts here can give a reasonable indication of changes in population levels. In some cases where actual counts are impossible or not meaningful then other methods of gauging the population changes can be used. One such method is by monitoring any change in the geographical distribution of a species – a contraction in range suggests a decreasing population.

The easiest species to study are those that hang in exposed positions in caves, like Greater Horseshoe bats. They have been carefully studied in Britain for over forty years and the number of caves used and bats present have been recorded in detail. This study shows that there are now less of these bats using less sites in a smaller range than when the study commenced; historical accounts indicate that this decline has been occurring since at least the turn of the century but has been escalating in recent years. Now there are only hundreds left in England whereas there used to be tens of thousands, and the distribution of this species is restricted to parts of south-west England and South Wales. This species also seems to be declining in Europe as do the Lesser Horseshoe and the Mouse-eared bats. Monitoring the numbers of other species that roost in less exposed sites is difficult but again studies suggest declining numbers and deserted roost sites.

Internationally the picture looks equally gloomy. Populations of some of the fruit bats are quite easy to assess as they roost in exposed positions in trees or in big, lofty caves. As human populations increase they cut down more forest for fuel, for land to grow crops and for space to build houses. As the forest disappears, the numbers of bats decline. In this way the numbers of bats on some small tropical islands have decreased alarmingly in recent years.

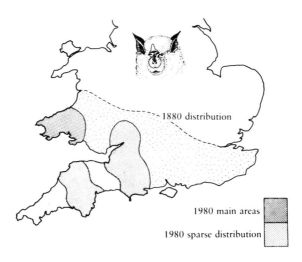

The decline of the Greater Horseshoe Bat in Britain (after R.E. Stebbings).

Habitat destruction is not the only reason for major changes in numbers of bats. At the famous Carlsbad Caverns in New Mexico, USA, the huge roost of Mexican Free-tailed bats has long drawn crowds of incredulous spectators. In the 1930s it was estimated that 8 million bats used the caves, but 20 years later the number had halved and now there are less than a million. This disastrous decline seems to be closely linked with the widespread use of DDT, which would be introduced into the food chain.

The Bat Conservation Trust in Britain has instigated a standardised monitoring programme for many of the more regularly found bats – a mixture of standard walks in randomly selected areas of habitat and roost counts. Bat detectors are used extensively to help this monitoring. By using repeatable methods, counts in ten years' time will more accurately pinpoint change. More precise methods for determining changes in population levels of the secretive species of bat are constantly being sought, and, with the help of new technology, it is hoped that declines in numbers will be quickly noticed so that remedial action can be taken.

Marking bats

Anyone with a garden and an interest in feeding the birds will almost certainly have noticed oddly marked birds appearing from time to time – a Blackbird with a white patch of feathers, a sparrow with a white tail feather or perhaps a Robin with a damaged leg. Your attention is always attracted and it is easy to see how long the bird stays in the area. Some of the mysteries of the lives of bats can be more closely examined by distinctly marking individuals. It is then possible to see how long a bat lives in the wild, how regularly it returns to a roost site, or a certain position in that roost site, where it moves to during the year, where it feeds and how it behaves socially in a roost. Unfortunately marking bats is not easy but methods have been developed to gather different information.

Banding

This involves attaching a light metal ring engraved with a serial number, a method first used in the USA in 1916, but now greatly improved. A well tried design used in Britain is a 'C'-clip, the smoothed ends of which bend outwards to prevent any damage to the wing membrane when it is lightly clipped over the forearm. A disadvantage is that bats include the clip in their toiletry and sometimes groom it so vigorously that the numbers become illegible; most, however, last the lifetime of the bat. Such permanent rings have been used to great effect to tell how long bats live and how far they move: merely by checking the ring numbers inside a roost annually over several years to find out when and where the bats were first marked (records of ring numbers are kept centrally).

Different coloured plastic rings have also been used; they have the

Bat 'rings' or 'bands'.

advantage of identifying an individual without having to disturb it. When I was studying the behaviour of Daubenton's bats inside a roost site during the night the comings and goings were most confusing – a bit like Platform 1 in the rush hour – until a bat that I had marked with a red ring appeared. Its movements were very easy to follow and made some sense out of the madness: it tried to join up with one group of snoozing bats but was chased off, it hung alone for a while, then tried a different group and so on. It would have been nice to know whether it was a male or female that drove it off each time and marking would have helped to discover this.

An ideal ring would have a serial number and also be coloured. This has been tried, using ordinary bands and painting them or covering in reflective tape. It works successfully but for only a limited time because the sharp little teeth of a grooming bat will remove any covering within a week or two. Some of my painted rings have lasted over a year but many last less than twenty-four hours. Colouring rings by anodizing will last longer but the colours are less bright.

Reflective tape
Small circles of different-coloured reflective tape can be lightly stuck to the wing membrane or body fur or even onto the wing band. A strong spotlight will pinpoint bats marked in this way as they fly past so one can study feeding ranges and night-time activity. They will only remain in place for a short period and will be removed as soon as the bat grooms.

Lights
Beta-lights consist of gas contained in a small phial which glows with a pale ghostly green light for many years. The light is not bright enough to see clearly unless the bat flies close so it may be necessary to use an expensive 'night-vision scope' (an electronic light-intensifier) to detect the feeble glow. Another technique is to use chemi-luminescent tags which contain chemicals that emit quite a bright green light for a few hours. Both types will be removed by the bats within a few days but can be useful for following bats from their roost sites to feeding grounds. An LED is a very small but bright light that is powered by a battery. If it is to be carried by a bat then the whole package must be very light in weight, so miniature batteries are used. An advantage is that they can be made to flash at different speeds and different colours can be used, which enables a number of individuals to be identified as they fly around. The brightness and the flashing makes them more noticeable from a distance. The bats may not appreciate the flashing, however, when they return to the roost site – what should be a dark, quiet haven becomes more

like a disco. Obviously the batteries have to be carefully chosen so that they go flat after a number of hours and so turn the lights off.

Radio tracking

Using any visual marking method such as lights has its limitations when tracking bats in flight as they soon sneak behind a tree or flit behind a building so are lost from sight. A more effective marking method is by using small radio transmitters. These can be as light as 0.5 g. and so can be stuck to the bats' backs without affecting them and will bleep away for days until their batteries run down. You do need a radio receiver to hear the bleeps, but can pick them up at ¾ mile (a kilometre) or more. The aerial on the special receiver pinpoints the direction of the bat and so roosting places can be discovered and night-time activities carefully followed. The problem is that the equipment is very expensive, with receivers costing £400 or more, and even the smallest transmitters are still rather bulky for our smaller bats to carry with comfort. Tracking of Greater Horseshoe bats with this method has been most successful and helped our understanding of the extent of feeding areas as well as locating inaccessible roosting sites.

Any work involving marking bats needs special training to prevent the bat suffering any distress and also a special NCC licence.

How long does a bat live?

A number of bats die in their first year. A bat's life is full of dangers for the helpless and inexperienced. Babies die if they obtain insufficient milk or if they fall from their lofty roosting places. Juveniles find that learning to fly and catching insects in flight is not easy; some never learn. Others begin hibernation without enough body fat to last through the winter so never wake to see the spring. Once a bat is over a year old then its survival chances

improve greatly. We have discovered by marking bats with numbered metal bands, that they can live to be over 20 years old. In Canada Little Brown bats have lived to be 30. Other records include

	age (years)
Greater Horseshoe	31
Lesser Horseshoe	18
Mouse-eared bat	22
Daubenton's bat	20
Pipistrelle	16

One reason that has been

suggested for the long life of such small creatures is that they spend a large slice of their lives torpid and this may slow down the process of ageing. Although a fascinating theory, it should be pointed out that fruit bats also live to be 20 or 30 and they cannot become torpid.

Whatever the reason (or perhaps it is the reason) the relatively small numbers of bats in a colony that reach sexual maturity and successfully rear a youngster each year makes long life essential if the population is to be maintained.

Ageing a bat that has not been marked in some way is almost impossible after the first year. Juvenile bats can be told from adults in the first few months of active life because they are slightly smaller, the wing membranes are soft and rubbery, the finger bones have not developed proper knuckles at the joints, but merely taper, and the body fur is greyer. Most species lose these characteristics in the ensuing six months. The state of the reproductive organs and the wear on the teeth provide further indications but plenty of experience is required with each species to be able to interpret these signs.

Causes of death

Some bats live to a ripe old age but others are not so fortunate in the savage world where creatures rely on each other to provide the next meal. Unlike many other animals, however, bats have no major predators. In Britain a few are caught by opportunistic birds of prey which may be passing and think a bat might make a tasty snack. Kestrel, Hobby, Sparrowhawk and owls all try to catch bats but none makes a living out of it – other prey are much easier to capture. Weasels and stoats sneak into all sorts of places and will eat a bat if the chance arises: in caves some bats hibernate almost at ground level and are well within reach of these voracious animals. The animal that catches and kills more bats than any other is the domestic cat. Living in and around houses, cats are certain to come into contact with many bat roosts. Some of the high-pitched calls of bats are audible to the sensitive hearing of cats and seem to attract or even irritate them. The cat is the only mammal likely to be found on rooftops with sufficient skill to snatch a bat out of the air as it flies past. Cats also wait just above or below a roost exit where the catching is easier.

Once whilst counting bats emerging from a roof I had to hang precariously out of an upstairs window on my back in order to look up towards the roost entrance a few feet higher. As the bats began to emerge I nearly lost my balance from the shock of a large furry face that suddenly appeared over the edge of the roof glaring down maliciously. It was a huge tomcat which then leant over and began to swipe at emerging bats. Fortunately I managed to shoo it away before any damage was done. Cats may catch bats but they do not usually eat them, just maul them – often fatally. From the cats' point of view bats are of minor importance as prey items, well below mice, birds, voles and shrews in popularity. From the bats' point of view cats are quite a worry. A few other creatures 'have a go' at bats such as crows and gulls. These bully-birds may chase a bat that has come out before dark but it seems more of a game for the birds rather than a hunt to the death.

Most bats die from natural causes or natural disasters. They suffer ill-health in the same way as other mammals and any weakness may prove fatal when the weather conditions are severe. The state of the weather has a major effect on all aspects of bats' lives. It can provide or deny insect food, make a hibernation site acceptable or otherwise and slow down or speed up the development of the young. Severe weather will kill the weak, the sick, the young and the old. Other natural causes of death can be a result of the type of roosting place chosen: caves and mines are likely to flood or have roof falls,

Pipistrelles leaving roost in the wall of an old stone-built thatched cottage; cats are one of a bat's worst enemies.

both of which may kill bats directly or block exit routes preventing escape; old buildings collapse, stone walls tumble and trees blow over, all of which may contain bats.

Unnatural deaths occur too frequently; poisoning by eating contaminated insects or by entering attics treated for woodworm (see Conservation) kills an unknown number each year. Bats are very sensitive to poisons, more so than other mammals that have been tested. Another cause for concern is the cavity wall insulation of houses. The gap between the inner and outer walls provides a cool and moist site which bats may use for hibernation. Many house-holders have this gap pumped full of insulating material to try to cut down on the heat loss from the house. Those bats that are not entombed within may find all their exits blocked. Unfortunately it is usually impossible to know if bats are present or not in a cavity wall. In my neighbouring village a young lady contacted me because she had a bat in her living room. Normally, she said, her husband would be there to take it outside but he was away for a week so could I go round? The following night the same thing happened with a second bat in the living room and again on the third night – except on this occasion the husband arrived home when I was upstairs with his wife looking for the bats' entry hole. It transpired that cavity wall insulation had recently been inserted, the bats had been trapped and had desperately searched for a way out. They had finally found a small hole in the wall around the waste pipe of a bathroom basin and from there had wandered around the house. Why each ended up in the living room is a real mystery (and so was the sudden appearance of the husband). Other summer and winter roosting sites are lost when entrances are unwittingly blocked and a subsequent decline in population seems inevitable. Some bats are trapped and die from starvation, others are excluded and have no other suitable site to use.

Accidents: well, they do happen, even to bats. Some are killed by cars on the road, particularly where the road is bordered by high hedgerows or by woodland which may be a good hunting ground for a bat. Some bats may only be stunned by a collision and live to flight another day. A colleague hit a bat and decided to stop and collect the corpse for me to look at. He threw the body onto the back seat of his car and drove off. After a few miles the bat came alive and began to flutter around inside the car causing the driver to stop quickly and get out even more quickly; the bat then made good its escape. Some road accidents are caused by a moment's lapse of attention by the bat or by the fast movement of vehicles but sometimes the accidents are hard to explain. An acquaintance was driving past a wood when a bat flew out and he hit it. This upset him and he slowed to below 30 m.p.h. and promptly collided with a second bat. This was just too much so he braked to a halt and in doing so a third bat flew out and bounced off his car apparently unhurt. Such clumsy behaviour is a real mystery, but one possible reason was suggested after my bat group was batting in a village; each member was outside a different roost site, and all were linked by walkie-talkies so that we could monitor what was happening at each roost as the bats flew out. During the

evening one of the team was amazed by a Pipistrelle that tried to catch the knobbly end of the long, whippy aerials of the transmitters, and ended up sliding down the aerial onto her hand before flying off. Since then we have successfully lured many a bat with the wobbly aerial trick. This, then, is one possible solution to some mysterious road accidents – car aerials may attract bats because the end appears to be an insect. There have even been some reports of bats impaled on car aerials.

Fatal accidents occur off the road, too, and pilot error is one cause. I have known bats to 'trip up' on clothes lines in gardens. Bats also become impaled on barbed wire. The last of these that I encountered was still alive and was successfully released with nothing more than a few holes in a wing. With such an excellent echo-location system, how are such accidents possible? Some are just sheer carelessness – looking the wrong way at the wrong time. Additionally bats get to know a feeding area very well and always follow the same flight path. If anything new obstructs that path then problems occur. When watching bats along a canal I was standing under a canal bridge with other group members when a Daubentons's Bat hurtled round the side of the bridge like a bat out of hell and flew straight into one of the team. It bounced off, landed on the ground then groggily took to flight again. Presumably it regularly flies under that bridge but this time the way was blocked.

Bats get into all kinds of scrapes and it is surprising that more do not get themselves killed. One Pipistrelle that I saved from certain death was at a factory. It had been trying to squeeze over the top corner of a partition wall and slipped so that its body slid down one side of the wall and its wing down the other side. The more it struggled the further down it slipped and the more tightly it became wedged. The factory manager noticed the bat (it was in his office) and contacted me – two weeks later. He thought it might be hibernating so had believed it best to leave it. Using levers I managed to free the bat after an hour and, amazingly, it was not only still alive but undamaged. It was given a drink and happily flew off into the night.

Disease

Bats, like other mammals, suffer from a wide range of diseases, few of which are ever passed on to man, and then only rarely. The disease that worries most people is rabies, yet the chance of anyone ever contacting this disease from a bat is extremely remote – there is more chance of being struck by lightning. In areas where rabies still exists other mammals such as dogs are more likely to pass it to humans. Some of the vampire bats in some parts of Central and South America do suffer from rabies and may infect any livestock on which they feed. Man is unlikely to be affected because he is not one of the vampire's preferred sources of food. Bat researchers may come into close contact if they are catching bats in these areas but the bats are not a major problem to the local populace. Livestock deaths occur at times and in parts of South America extreme action to limit this loss in revenue has resulted in the dynamiting of bats and their roosts – many thousands of Brazilian caves, for instance, were destroyed in three years for this reason. Few of the bats that were killed were vampires, most were innocent victims of this pointless action. Of those vampires that were killed not all carried the disease anyway. More selective methods are now being used in those areas where treatment is necessary although cave destruction continues. Rabies is absent from Britain; so there is no need whatever for alarm here. Even in Europe, where rabies is present in wildlife, bats are not a threat and do not carry the disease.

Another disease problem associated with bats is histoplasmosis – but it is not really anything to do with the bats at all. It is a disease of the lungs caused by inhaling spores from a fungus which lives in soil but is more prevalent in the rich guano under a large bat (or bird) roost. Again the problem is very limited: it is more often encountered in caves in tropical areas. Bat researchers or guano-collectors are the only ones at risk.

Since few other health risks seem to be associated with bats, little research has been carried out on the effects that other diseases have on the bats themselves. As with most diseases in mammals, few are fatal and most bats seem able to make a good recovery. If, however, the disease causes a weakening at a sensitive time of the year (e.g. at the start or end of hibernation), then the chances of survival will be lowered.

Bats should not be feared as disease-carriers. There is little evidence to show that they cause us any harm. Here in Britain the mammal to fear for spreading disease is our fellow man. Bats are innocent.

Parasites

Parasites (in case you are scratching your head wondering – these are organisms that usually live entirely on another life form and gain all their nourishment from it) are found on the surface and inside all mammals including man. In Britain fleas, lice and bed-bugs still affect many people although less so now than before Victorian times when they were an everyday part of life. Our dogs and cats are commonly affected by fleas, too. My neighbour was bemoaning the fact that his prize pedigree dog was infested with fleas again. I asked him where the dog had picked them up from; 'Search me,' he said in all innocence. Bats have their share of parasites. I'm sure that you are itching to find out more about them. The internal parasites are 'worms' of various types and single-celled organisms that live in the blood. External parasites ('ectoparasites') have had to adapt specially to scratch a living on the surface of a bat's body. The main types of ectoparasites are bat-flies, bat-bugs, mites, fleas and ticks.

Bats are very clean animals and groom themselves

fastidiously so the ectoparasites have had to adapt to avoid being groomed off. They either run or hop out of the way when the grooming is taking place or they hang on very tightly with special claws to avoid being scratched off. Some live in or on the body fur, others prefer the bare areas of skin, especially the wing membrane. It takes a very special kind of creature to be able to stay in place on a bat's wing when it is flying: you would think the rapid up and down movement and the air rushing by would dislodge them. The special adaption of these parasites is one reason why very few are ever found on any other mammal, and some are restricted to living on only one type of bat. This means that it is not possible for bat parasites to move onto humans – we are just not suitable habitats for them.

Some of these sweet little hitch-hikers carry out their whole life cycle (eggs, larvae, pupae/nymph, adult stage) on board a bat; some only spend their adulthood there, and others hop on for a feed, then jump off again before the bat flies out of the roost site. Their main food is a little blood which is taken by jabbing the mouthparts through the bat's skin and sucking. Some mites, however, eat skin fragments.

Generally bats should not be thought of as lousy animals – I have seen more ecto-parasites on a human being than I have on any bat in Britain. Some species are comparatively free from parasites and those that are affected will often only have visible signs during that part of the year when the parasite is in its larval or adult stage.

Sick, injured and orphaned bats

The commonest cause of injury to bats brought to me for treatment is mauling by cats. The damage often involves torn or holed wing membranes, broken forearms or fingers or internal damage. The wing membrane begins to show signs of healing after about a week with pink scar tissue forming at the edge of the damage. Small holes pucker at the edges as the membrane is pulled inwards and soon the hole heals over completely; large holes become smaller. A torn membrane is more of a problem as it is very difficult to make the torn parts knit together again. Broken fingers cause little problem because they are wholly held within the membrane that gives them support. The broken ends need to be realigned and carefully taped over to hold them in position until the bones re-join. Broken forearms can be re-set successfully by pinning but this is quite a skilled task and best carried out by a vet. Whilst the bone is healing it is important that the bat does not attempt to use its wing so it should be lightly and firmly bound, and the bat kept in a small cage to limit its movements. Unfortunately bats walk about using their wrists as supports, and this will put strain on the fractured forearm; sometimes a splint of wood (a matchstick) on the forearm can ease the strain.

As soon as the bat sees the bandages it will busily remove them with its teeth, so it is usually necessary to fit the bat with a small card collar to prevent this. A fracture on the forearm close to the wrist is very difficult to repair, as are breaks in the upper arm (humerus) and thigh bone (femur) as they are partly hidden inside the bat's body. In such cases the advice of a vet should be sought and if repair is impossible then amputation may be necessary, so making the bat a permanent but disabled pet. Broken bones are not always easy to diagnose. One Pipistrelle brought in to me for treatment could only fly with difficulty and apparent distress. Its wings were undamaged but the membrane is, of course, attached to the back legs and close examination showed that the femur was broken and was put under strain whenever the bat flew. Internal damage is neither easy to diagnose nor to repair. Puncture marks on the body should be carefully located, the surrounding hair cut away and the damaged skin treated with warm water and mild antiseptic.

Whiskered Bat with bandaged arm and card-collar to prevent him tearing the bandage off.

Sick bats
Little is known of the illnesses of bats but they seem similar to those that afflict other mammals so should be treated in the same way. Much can be done by merely providing safe, warm, quiet accommodation with ample food and water, so giving natural processes a better chance of curing injury or illness. Again a vet may be helpful with specific advice and can supply antibiotics which will help in a number of cases.

Care and maintenance
Patients are best kept in small cages of untreated wood or plastic with mesh or card linings to provide ample hanging space. A removable partition will provide a crevice behind which they can squeeze. A shallow dish of water on the floor of the cage provides necessary liquid for the bats and also improves humidity. The floor can be lined with paper to facilitate cleaning. The patient should be kept warm (25°–30°C) and quiet at all times (an airing cupboard can be ideal). The warmth helps to keep the bat active and seems to speed up the healing process. As in a real hospital, it is important to keep a daily record of progress – food taken, medicines administered and the weight of the patient: the latter is a helpful guide to the condition of the bat.

It is impractical to try to supply a bat with the same types and quantities of insects that it would obtain in the wild. Nutritious alternatives that have been

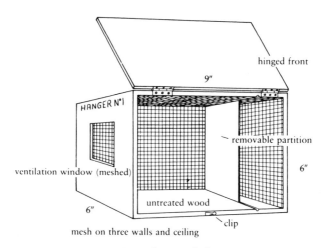

Cage for poorly bat.

tried include mashed hard-boiled egg and tinned cat food. The main food that all bats love is the mealworm which is the larva of a beetle. Mealworms can be obtained from pet shops and, although rather expensive, are a real treat and are rarely refused by a bat. A Pipistrelle will need about 10-15 mealworms a day and larger bats will require proportionally more. At first the patient needs to be encouraged to eat this novel food and this is best achieved by smearing some of the juicy insides of a mealworm onto the bat's lips. Eventually they can be trained to take mealworms from a dish in the cage. Small amounts of vitamin and mineral powder should be added to supplement the diet. Liquids are important and water should be always available, particularly at meal-times. Bats can be encouraged to drink by dipping the tips of their snouts into a drop of water on a spoon. It seems sensible to regularize mealtimes to coincide with dusk each day, a time when bats are usually active.

Exercise is a major problem for injured bats. Broken bones prevent the chance of exercise by flying and so it is important to ensure that the bat does not become overweight, by carefully regulating its diet. As soon as the bat has regained its health then it should be encouraged to fly in a closed room, preferably at mealtimes when it is active, so as to get it fit again. A large living room is ideal as the soft furnishings cushion any crash landings. Ensure that the bat cannot creep behind any immovable object or it may take a long time to entice it out again. An injured Whiskered Bat in my care managed to find a small crevice behind my staircase and I only managed to recapture it by shifting the entire staircase a few inches to one side and dangling a mealworm on a cotton thread into the crevice – the bat bit and I reeled it in. Usually a half-hour flight will give the bat plenty of exercise, but always watch where it goes because a bat can hide very successfully in any room.

Orphans

Baby bats are often found under a roost site in June and July and the best solution is to return them immediately up into the roost as long as the adult bats are still using the site. Rearing orphans is difficult and time-consuming. They require regular small amounts of milk (not creamy or fatty milk) fed directly into their mouths through a small plastic pipette or eye-dropper. In their cages they must be kept warm at all times as this encourages growth (see previous section) and also is vital in digestion: a cold baby with a belly full of milk cannot digest it. When the permanent teeth have grown it is time to begin to wean them onto more solid foods such as the insides of mealworms. Throughout the rearing, a small amount of powdered vitamins and minerals can be added to the food. When in their cage they appreciate a 'mother substitute' and a small strip of fur hung up will quickly be used. Even adult bats appreciate these furry strips and always like to snuggle into them. Young bats can then be encouraged to fly in a closed room, and when they can navigate proficiently will be ready for release.

Release time

It is only too easy to become hopelessly attached to captive bats so when the time comes for their discharge many a tear is shed. Unfortunately bats rarely live long in captivity so you should release them as soon as possible. It is vital that they are released at the place where they were acquired (preferably into a roost), at dusk and only when the weather is reasonable and other bats are flying. Hopefully they will soon find all the roost sites and feeding areas that they once knew and take their place back in bat society again.

Bats and the law

In 1981 a new Act of Parliament, the Wildlife and Countryside Act, gave protection to all bats in Britain and to their roost sites. This brought Britain into line with wildlife protection laws of most other European countries and improved on many. There are three main areas of protection:

1. Preventing assault and battery. It is illegal to intentionally kill or injure any bat, but then you wouldn't want to. Not everyone is as thoughtful and understanding and this has led to a number of unnecessary bat deaths in the past. Such persecution has been a serious threat to the continued survival of rare species.

2. Combating disturbance. It is illegal to disturb a bat at roost. This covers all roost sites such as caves, trees, buildings and even your own house if bats are present. Even when we are being as quiet as possible near roosting bats we are still making a number of high frequency sounds every time we move – brushing a nylon jacket against a wall, scraping a shoe on a gritty floor and even whispering, all contain their quota of high-pitched sounds. Although we cannot hear much of this noise, the bats certainly can as their hearing is especially sensitive to it, and they soon wake up. Another unintentional disturbance is the heat from our bodies, which can cause the cool air of a cave to rise in temperature; even a slight temperature increase can cause the bats to awake. Cigarette smoke also disturbs and disturbance of any kind during hibernation or when young are present can cause premature death (see p. 42), but at all times there is a real risk of the bats feeling that their roosting site is no longer safe and so deserting it.

3. Stopping roost site battering. It is illegal to damage a roost site or obstruct the entrance. This is another very important part of the Act. There is no point in protecting bats and then finding that they have nowhere to live. The entrances are often insignificant slots or gaps in a house roof or wall and it is very important to ensure that these are never blocked. Imagine coming back to your house and finding the doorway sealed up and, to make it worse, some of your relatives and children inside unable to get out.

'But,' you are thinking, 'if the Englishbat's home is now his castle and no repairs can be carried out because of the problem of disturbance, surely the building will eventually fall down and the bats will lose their roost site anyway.' There is provision in the Act to cater for just such problems, and in cases where maintenance work is to be carried out or the bats are to be disturbed in any way then the Nature Conservancy Council (NCC) must be informed and asked for advice. This is the Government body that promotes nature conservation and it has special responsibility for the Act. The council can suggest ways in which the proposed work may be carried out with the least bat disturbance. It is essential that it is consulted and only it can give the special permission necessary (for address, see Information). If people don't like bats and don't want them the NCC advises how to solve the problem. Bat workers, of course, are also controlled by the Act and are only allowed to catch or mark bats, enter roost sites or even photograph bats if they have a very good reason to do so and have been granted a special Government licence.

If a bat enters the living area of your house then you are allowed to pick it up carefully and put it back outside. Some bats do make mistakes when navigating at night and occasionally enter an open window; they are very keen to be helped to find their way outside again and have no plans to turn your bedroom into a de-luxe bat roost. You can also handle an injured bat in order to tend it and help it as much as is necessary, but otherwise you need a licence to handle a bat.

Penalties for contravening the law can be costly and fines up to £2,000 are possible for every bat killed, for instance. Strict laws, but will they help? The Protection of Wild Creatures Act of 1975 gave equal protection to the Greater Horseshoe and Mouse-eared bats, and also made it necessary to obtain a licence before marking bats. The Mouse-eared Bat is now extinct in Britain and the numbers of Greater Horseshoe bats still seem to be declining. Laws in themselves can only have limited effect. Changes in public attitudes to bats will be more productive.

Bat 'problems' and what to do about them

The problems are really caused by people not bats. Bats live normal, natural lives but, if in close contact with man, produce some complaints. This chapter concerns the conflict that occurs from time to time. The bat-tle ground is usually a building used by human beings, which the bats have also carefully selected as a home. Instead of feeling honoured by having the little lodgers some people are downright aggressive, but much of this nastiness is caused by a lack of knowledge about bats. The 'problems' fall into two main categories – fear or uncertainty about bats and the mess left by their droppings.

Fear

The many myths about bats (see Bat Myths) certainly give the wrong impression about our furry friends. People are often wary or frightened of bats just through ignorance of these mysterious black shapes that flit around the garden at night. At some roosts I have visited with 'problems' the man of the house has told me that he quite likes bats, but it's his wife . . . and the kids of course . . . that are really frightened. Later the wife has taken me to one side and said that she has always been secretly fond of bats, but it's her husband who has an aversion to them . . . and the kids of course. Meanwhile I find that the kids adore bats and want to keep them as pets. In fact when those people with reservations have been given a chance to look closely at a bat in the hand then loathing usually turns to loving and they always comment on how small and cuddly bats look. Such people, who would willingly have evicted the bats from their houses before they knew anything about them, now carefully guard the roosts and keep a close check on the comings and goings each season. One lady even rang me up in tears one day because her bats had failed to arrive back that year; at our initial meeting she had asked about the quickest way to kill those bats. A bit of education, then, saves many a bat roost and informative visits to roost-owners can quickly allay any fears. This is, perhaps, one of the more important conservation roles of local bat groups.

Real phobias do exist and are far more difficult to conquer than the fear of the unknown. A phobia can affect others in close contact, especially impressionable children. One dear old lady discovered that a few Pipistrelles were roosting under the eaves of her house. She had a real deep-seated fear of bats and other flying creatures. Her immediate precautions to prevent any possibility of a bat entering her house involved locking all doors just before dusk and bolting them securely, closing all windows and drawing the curtains and bolting and padlocking the hatchway into the loft. No sprigs of garlic around the entrances but just about everything else to try to set her mind at rest. She was still having problems sleeping at night so her daughter called us in to offer advice. The mother would not be influenced by any arguments and, although the daughter said she thought her mother was being a little silly, she was herself quite affected by the strong feelings of her mother. This was apparent when she agreed to come outside with us to locate the roost entrance but then made a dash for her car, leapt inside, locked the doors, wound up the windows and even closed the ventilators. We then had to lip-read as she indicated the roost position. In this case the bats fortunately left a few days later so no drastic action was needed.

Droppings
Although harmless, they can be messy in some situations and so cause more bat/human conflict. Most problems of this nature concern droppings from large roosts of Pipistrelles which accumulate under the roost entrance outside a house. Often garden or tarmac hide the signs but occasionally ledges, doorsteps or vehicles may be directly in the line of fire. The bats are in residence for only a short period of time so it seems pointless to take drastic action, and in many cases a little thought can ease the mess problem considerably. In one case a snow-white caravan was parked directly beneath the roost and was rapidly becoming Dalmatian-like, much to the annoyance of the owner. The problem was solved simply by shifting the caravan a few feet to one side. Plastic covers are another cheap and simple solution to a messy problem.

Damage to property
Another concern of some householders when they see bats entering their roofs is possible damage to woodwork or electrical wiring as can be caused by other mammals such as rats, mice and squirrels by gnawing. Bats only use existing slots or holes and if the apertures do not suit then they go elsewhere – they never gnaw or enlarge holes. A quick glance at the teeth of bats will show that they are not designed for gnawing.

Other problems
Other problems occur from time to time. Some people object to the pattering of tiny feet in the attic, and the odd batty aroma has caused a few wrinkled noses. Bats flying around inside castles, warehouses or shops at night have

triggered burglar alarm systems. At one house-roost I visited, the owner's car, parked nearby, had its windscreen covered in grubby little footprints as the bats apparently clambered around looking for squashed insects. These isolated problems can usually be solved with a little ingenuity.

Overall the problems are few and not really serious, and most can be solved without disturbing the bats at all; it must always be remembered that they are very sensitive creatures and eviction from a roost site is likely to cause their deaths. Such extreme action must only be taken as a very last resort and then only with the agreement of the NCC. For advice, contact your local bat group (see Information).

Would you evict bats from your house?

The usefulness of bats

'What use are bats?' is a commonly asked question. Bats fit into very complex sets of relationships with other forms of life that find the bats essential rather than just useful for their continued existence. Often the questioner is trying to discover, however, how useful bats are to *us* and is less concerned with the fate of associated plants, insects and other creatures. Some bats help man directly and, naturally enough, much interest has been shown in those species. In other countries, the nectar-eating bats pick up pollen on their fur as they move from flower to flower and are major pollinators of many trees and plants. Fruit bats help with seed-dispersal. Such bats have been found to be instrumental in the spread and continued survival of over 1,000 species of tree, some of which are important to the natives of the area as a food or fuel supply and also for trade. Bats help to disperse seeds of such important crops as mangoes, peaches, avocadoes and figs. The insectivorous bats, like those in Britain, are not idle – they eat vast numbers of insects each night. Some of these insects are pests to our crops, forests, buildings and ourselves.

Bats are taken for food by natives in Africa and Asia; the bat population can cope with the limited predation when they only collect enough for themselves and their families. Unfortunately bats have become a delicacy in

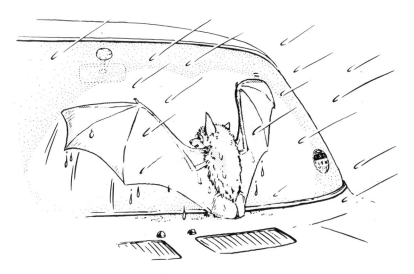

The uses of bats – windscreen-wipers.

some areas and this has resulted in large numbers being caught in nets and sold for profit. Such pressures have caused local extinctions. Bats may be useful for food but more useful for growing food because their droppings make excellent fertilizer. Accumulations from large roosts in caves in the tropics are collected and sold, and a number of communities rely on the income for their continued existence.

Parts of bats are used in the preparation of medicines in some places in the East. The effectiveness of such preparations has yet to be proved. The best tonic for me would be to see no bats used in such concoctions.

Bats have also proved useful for research of all sorts. Their extremely effective echo-location system is being closely studied to help the development of navigational aids. Another important field of research is the study of the complex breeding cycle with its delayed implantation and delayed fertilization, which is of interest to those studying various aspects of human and livestock breeding.

Details of the lives of many bats are little known. Doubtless further 'uses' will be discovered in the future. I believe that such uses are a bonus; we shouldn't require a use. Bats exist: they are part of our complex natural world, in which each creature has an important position. Without them our world would be a poorer place.

Myths

For thousands of years, bats have been connected with the affairs of man and, naturally enough, many tales have arisen. Being rather secretive animals and difficult to observe, many of the tales have very little basis in fact: as bats are active at night, they have become linked in people's minds with ghosts, witches and demons, all of which were much feared by simple folk. Similar tales and superstitions developed around the owl, another innocent creature whose only crime is to be active at night. Even today many people believe that bad luck or death will result in a home if an owl perches on a house roof; worse would happen if it were to look at you. Horror movies have played on the uncertainties that are still felt about bats and they depict them as a frightening evil that will attack at any time. In our modern world superstitions are dying, but a rather slow death. Ludicrous stories are, unfortunately, still believed, however unlikely or unreasonable they are. Myths from ancient times are little remembered now, but mainly concerned the origin of bats and the links between bats and spirits. Some cultures feared bats as evil, others thought them signs of good fortune and bats were even worshipped in some areas. Recent myths about bats are commonly heard and still widely accepted as being true. A few examples are:

'As blind as a bat.' A widely used expression, but it is difficult to understand its origins. Even though we have only recently realized that bats 'see' with sound, anyone watching bats flying around at night must have realized that they can 'see' very well and carefully avoid objects in their path. All bats have obvious eyes, too, which they can use quite effectively, and our ancestors must have noticed them. It certainly was a puzzle to many people how the bats did see in the dark, but to describe them as blind is strange. Nevertheless the phrase has stuck.

'Bats fly into your hair.' Another commonly held belief that causes unnecessary worry to people at night. Reason should make one ask, 'Why should a bat fly into one's hair?' to which there is no answer. In fact an entangled bat would hate the experience (finding it hair-raising). How does such a saying arise if there is no truth in it? I think there are two main reasons for this myth. Firstly, bats are inquisitive animals and may swoop down low over anyone who walks in their feeding territory at night just to see what they are and if they constitute any danger. Secondly, we cannot see the large number of insects that we disturb in a night-time stroll and that follow us or fly up near us. In the daytime a column of gnats over someone's head is a far from uncommon sight but at night we are less aware of such happenings. Bats can detect the insects very easily and may fly close by to snap up this bonanza. At dusk it is quite easy to see the bat as it swoops close and the breeze from its wing beats will ruffle any hair-do. Such happenings probably put the idea into people's heads that the bat had landed. Doubtless someone, somewhere, has had a bat become entangled but it is a very rare occurrence and certainly an accident. I have met one lady who insists it happened to her when she was a little girl riding along on her bicycle sixty years ago. All the other reports that I have received (and there have been a number) were never first-hand accounts; they had always 'happened to a friend'. It is never possible to confirm such stories. The tales more often concern females, possibly due to their elaborate hair styles.

As part of my research I use very fine mist nets to try to catch bats in flight, with mesh almost as fine as human hair. The bats obviously detect the nets and have no trouble avoiding them, sometimes even flying along the top, then down each side to get a better look. If bats flew into ladies' hair then we would do away with our nets and take lots of ladies into the field with us.

'Bats in the belfry.' An expression referring to someone who is a little irrational in behaviour. The link with bats is hard to see. It makes people associate bats with belfries of churches and also with madness – neither of which is true. Although bats will feed in churchyards and often fly close to the church tower the belfry is not one of the favoured roosting sites (see Roosts).

Blood lust. In the 1500s word came back from explorers of Central and South America that there was a bat that drank blood living in the area. Since these times such stories have caught the imagination of many, even though they commonly experienced horse-flies, mosquitoes and other insects that drank their blood each summer. Bram Stoker's *Dracula* in 1897 got the ball rolling (or the blood flowing) and all sorts of weird and wonderful bats have been depicted with this sanguineous thirst. But back to the facts. There are three species of vampire bats, all living in South and Central America; they prefer to feed from cattle, horses or birds and rarely touch people. They take only a comparatively small amount of blood, so that they can return and feed again another night, so no empty cows lying like husks on the ground. The vampires have been persecuted and two of the species are quite rare. The biggest is only about 4 inches (10 cm.) long so hardly a thing to have nightmares about. Still, who bothers about facts when there are good films to believe in? At a Pipistrelle roost I visited in the heart of the English countryside the owner pointed to a headless corpse of a mouse on the lawn and blamed the bats, whilst his fat tomcat sat on the doorstep looking smug. Another amazing tale concerns a villager who was incredulous when we showed him a bat in daytime – he firmly believed that if the sun's rays hit it then it would go up in a puff of smoke.

Nest building, egg-laying etc. A more reasonable misconception. Unlike birds, however, bats use no nesting material or bedding but just enter a suitable roosting site and make do with that. They do not form pairs like birds but more complex social structures are involved. Bat eggs are also rather uncommon (see Breeding).

heh-heh-heh

Research

In Britain there are a few university departments involved in different aspects of bat research. They are looking at such things as behaviour, energy requirements, echo-location and the general ecology of bats at home and abroad. Some of the work is initiated by the Government-funded Nature Conservancy Council or the Institute of Terrestrial Ecology. Any form of research requires funding and nowadays there is tremendous competition for the little money available. Bats are not an economic or health problem in Britain and they don't attract money for research. An added problem is the great difficulty of studying these aerial and nocturnal mammals; research becomes very time-consuming. Research workers are financially limited in the time that they can spend on a project and the more complex projects might not be completed within the time and funds available. Nevertheless progress is slowly made, and each year our knowledge of the lives of bats gradually improves.

The research contribution of amateurs must not be forgotten. Much of our knowledge of the Greater Horseshoe Bat is due to the hard work of keen amateurs over the last forty years. Some small projects carried out by bat groups (see p. 118) are turning into major research programmes. My own bat group, for instance, has been studying Daubenton's bats for a number of years. We are looking particularly at nocturnal movements, feeding and

Studying the movements of bats.

social behaviour. Other groups are studying Pipistrelles and Natterer's bats in a similarly detailed way. Although amateur workers can only spend limited time on such studies, their enthusiasm for field work has produced a wealth of valuable data. The blossoming interest in bats in recent years makes the future of bat research look more rosy. We still know very little about the lives of most British species and a better understanding will aid effective conservation.

Much research is carried out in American universities, especially on bats in tropical areas of the New World. Canada, Australia and a number of European countries are also involved in some aspects of research.

As technology has made available lightweight radio-tracking devices (see Marking bats), image intensifiers, ultrasonic detectors, portable computer storage systems and similar apparatus, it has become possible to learn a lot about the secret ways of bats. New technology will, I am sure, enable us to discover yet more about the complex but fascinating lives of our furry friends.

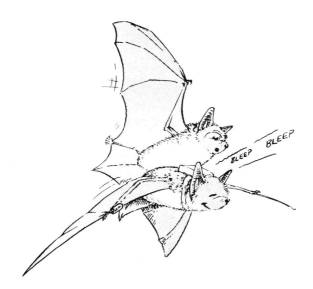

Bat projects

Some bat research is complicated and requires expensive equipment, but there are simple projects that the amateur bat worker can carry out and that provide interesting information, and, most importantly, do not disturb the bats so will not require special NCC licences to permit the work. Often local bat groups will be co-ordinating such activities and they should be approached for guidance; they will also be pleased to receive results of any project work.

Roost monitoring

The activities of bats at their roost sites are full of interest. One useful thing to do is watch when they come out in the evening. A position outside the roost needs to be chosen so that any emerging bat will be seen against the night sky. At house roosts this means standing almost underneath the exit hole at sunset and staring upwards. No lights should be used because they will affect the behaviour of the emerging bats.

First-emergence times: note down the time that the first bat emerges and the time of sunset. See how the time changes during the season and if activities inside the roost (such as when young can be heard) affect it.

Total number: most bats will have emerged within an hour after the first bat so this project merely requires counting the bats during this period. A bat detector (see p. 31) is a useful aid as each shadowy shape can be then heard as it flits out. A hand tally counter (a device, operated by a button, that keeps a running total) may also be useful at large roosts. The number emerging usually reaches a peak and then decreases again so it is quite apparent when the emergence has finished. Sometimes a few stay inside the roost site all night and can be heard chattering inside, but, when the weather is satisfactory, they will be very few in number (N.B. in June and July young may be present). It is interesting to see how the total number changes, so counts each week, or even more frequently if possible, will provide useful data.

Rate of emergence: the bats do not all emerge together but in peaks of activity. This may change during different months, particularly if young are present. Monitor the rate by counting how many bats emerge every five minutes throughout the total emergence time and then plot a graph of this number against time. Obviously the total number can be calculated from the figures too.

Period of use of roost site: many roost sites are used for quite short times and only in some months. Visiting the site twice a week after dusk will enable you to see if bats are emerging from the site and also will tell you when they have moved out. Don't abandon the site if the bats move out, but continue to visit it, because the bats may return a few weeks later. Many Pipistrelle roosts in houses can be more effectively and accurately monitored by placing a sheet of paper on the ground under the exit hole so that it will collect droppings as soon as bats begin to use the site. These should be cleared regularly and when they no longer appear you will know that the bats have gone.

Weather conditions may affect the activity or numbers at a site so it is worth recording details such as temperature, wind force and direction, cloud cover, rain and phase of the moon. Remember that insect numbers could be affected by the weather conditions of many days ago, so the first 'good' night of weather may have few insects because they are still struggling to pupate. Recent weather conditions may be as important as the weather that night.

Data loggers can now be purchased which automatically count the bats as they emerge through an infra-red beam or as they make a sound on a bat detector. At the end of the evening's emergence the information can be down-loaded into a personal computer and analysed fully. The exact time (to the second) of each bat's emergence will have been noted, so patterns of emergence rates can be shown. If the echo-location calls are recorded from a time-expansion bat detector they can be analysed by a simple piece of soft-ware in a PC and the individual calls analysed. We need to know the reason for each 'shout' – some are for finding insects, but are some for communicating with other bats?

Feeding and feeding areas

Although a little more difficult than monitoring roosts, some studies on feeding are possible.

Flight paths: as the bats set off from their roosts they tend to follow the same line of flight. Starting at the roost site on one night, follow the flight path on progressive nights to discover where the bats move to.

Feeding areas: individual bats fly backwards and forwards within one area. Try to plot the boundaries of their 'patch'. It is usually easier to carry out such work at a fairly open site such as a lake or parkland. Again, a bat detector makes such work easier.

Food: Sometimes bats can be seen taking individual insects from the surface of water or perhaps from a swarm over land. By collecting one or two of the insects it is possible to deduce which species have been selected. Unfortunately many items caught by the bats may be difficult for us to catch or too few in number to see. Studying the fragments in bat droppings remains the most successful method of identifying prey items (see Bat grub).

Bat boxes

Plenty of scope here for keen amateurs. Building and erecting the boxes is a project in itself (see p. 87) but it is important to check the boxes monthly to see if bats have used them. If not, then it might be a good idea to move them to a more suitable site (but leave them for a few years first, to blend in with surroundings). Careful records need to be kept of the location of the box, the design, the facing direction, height, etc. Any birds, nests or insects found in the boxes should also be recorded as they may influence future designs. Obviously the bats should not be disturbed unduly by the check so an experienced and licensed bat worker could be of assistance when you go. Bat box projects are best organized through a county bat group so that the boxes are erected in the most suitable areas. Often no bats will be present but sometimes their droppings will indicate that they have used the box. They may even breed there.

These are just a few examples of projects that individuals can carry out. If a team of people is involved then the work can be extended greatly. In most cases the first problem is to find the roosts, so initially the project should be to visit likely buildings and look for signs, such as droppings. Start with churches or church porches, which should produce a number of roosts and provide much experience in recognizing the signs of the presence of bats. All this work can be carried out in the daytime and all churches in an area can be visited by a small team. Once a suitable roost has been found then other project work can begin. It must always be remembered that no disturbance of bats is allowed, so only enter areas where bats will not be disturbed – caves, attics and similar roosts cannot be entered by unlicensed people if bats are present.

Fun of batting

Once you get involved with bats then studying their ways becomes engrossing. Finding out more about their life styles can be a real challenge and a lot of fun, and helping to conserve these endearing creatures produces enormous satisfaction.

Bats are mainly studied at night and this adds a certain mystique and excitement to the work. The locations of the roosts also add to the fun – awesome caves, eerie mansions and creepy churchyards. Even roosts in ordinary houses can be a great deal of fun because many of the roost-owners, who may

have gone out of their way to inform you of their roosts, are real characters. Some even hold bat parties. In summer the neighbours, friends and bat groupies are invited to the party on the patio with the food and drink all having a bat 'flavour' – bat-shaped biscuits and sandwiches, nuts labelled as bat droppings and the whisky labelled 'Bat 69'. By emergence time everyone is in a very merry mood, but this is the highlight of the whole evening and all noise stops except for the faint chattering of the bats deep inside their roost site. As they begin to emerge the counting begins. Obviously the state of some members present is not conducive to accurate counting but the interest is intense and all are desperately hoping that last year's total will be exceeded.

The problem is that few people ever have the opportunity to experience bats. In one village I had been asked to look at a roost under the eaves of a house. As soon as I began to set up my equipment neighbours' doors began opening and out they all came as the word quickly spread. By the time the bats began to emerge a crowd of at least thirty had formed in the road and watched as I used one of my special nets to capture one of the bats for identification. Once successful, I received my first round of applause. So many questions were being fired at me by this time that I decided to give a short public lecture on bats and their lives. Cars trying to move along this quiet street were unable to pass but the drivers just got out and joined the throng. The finale was the release of the bat, a Pipistrelle, which flew off to tumultuous applause and, being a real professional, gained a few gasps of amazement by dodging in and around branches of a tree. Some of the audience wanted to make a night of it and were re-emerging from their houses with mugs of soup and getting their children out of bed to join in the excitement. It was quite a disappointment when the last bat emerged and there was nothing else to see. The crowds thinned, the abandoned cars were claimed and village life reverted to normal.

Some of my most enjoyable moments have been watching bats and listening to them on a detector. The first time I heard a bat on a detector I was convinced of the importance of these machines for sensing bats. The sounds add to the picture of the shadowy shape that can be seen flitting around. At favourite feeding areas the large numbers of bats produce a tremendous rattle of sound on the detector as they excitedly chase after their food. Some sounds are beautiful: the first time I heard a Horseshoe bat left me spellbound – its rich warble of sound has to be heard to be believed. My idea of heaven is to sit at the edge of a small lake or pond at dusk in summer, watching and listening to the bats as they arrive to feed. Noctules fly high and always seem in a hurry, Pipistrelles at the water's edge busily snap up flies, then Daubenton's bats, silhouetted against the reflected glow of sunset, skim across the surface, occasionally circling round to catch a caddis fly. Just before dark the air is alive with bats, some chasing each other, others patrolling up and down, still more gathering around a mass of insects and swirling in amongst them with breathtaking agility. I could watch them for hours (and often do) until the remaining glimmer of light from the western sky fades into darkness.

Bat groups

These are groups of amateurs interested in research and in the conservation of bats. Bat groups are mostly county based and are found in all areas of England and Wales with smaller numbers in Scotland and Ireland. Many are closely connected with the county Wildlife Trusts. Bat Groups send representatives to regional meetings and regional representatives meet regularly with others involved with bats from national, international and government bodies. This is co-ordinated by the Bat Conservation Trust, a membership organization aiming to conserve bats through education and study. Members of a group are the accepted experts in that area and will be licensed to work with bats. They carry out a variety of different conservation and research projects such as monitoring population levels, feeding activity, species distribution, surveying hibernacula and roost types and giving protection, and caring for sick or injured bats. A very important part of their work involves educating people about bats through roost visits, public lectures and publicity. Whatever your interest in bats, it is worth contacting your local group. The address can be obtained from your local Wildlife Trust (see telephone directory) or the Bat Conservation Trust.

Further reading

Detailed studies have been published in scientific journals; copies of such journals can be obtained through the public library service if full details of the title of the article, author and journal are provided. Lists of studies are given in the references or bibliographies of books dealing with bats (e.g. *Handbook of British Mammals*).

Few books have been written specifically about British bats, most concern worldwide bats. The following books will be of greatest interest to British bat enthusiasts. Some are now out of print but can be obtained at some second-hand bookshops or borrowed through libraries.

British bats

Arnold, H.R., *Atlas of Mammals of Britain* (Biological Records Centre, Monks Wood Experimental Station, Abbots Ripton, Huntingdon, 1993)

Corbet, G.B., & S. Harris (eds), *Handbook of British Mammals* (Blackwell Scientific, Oxford, 1991)

Schober, W., & E. Grimmberger, *A Guide to the Bats of Britain and Europe* (Hamlyn, London, 1993)

Focus on Bats is a booklet about bats and the law obtainable from English Nature (see p.126)

Worldwide bats

Altringham, J.D., *Bats: Biology and Behaviour* (Oxford University Press, 1996)

Fenton, M.B., *Bats* (Facts on File, New York, 1992)

Hill, J.E. & J.D. Smith, *Bats: A Natural History* (British Museum Natural History, London, 1984)

Nowak, R.M., *Walker's Bats of the World* (The John Hopkins University Press, Baltimore and London, 1994)

Thompson, S., & P. Richardson, *Bat Conservation Project Book* (Hodder & Stoughton, Sevenoaks, 1993)

Yalden, D.W., & P.A. Morris, *The Lives of Bats* (David and Charles, Newton Abbot, 1975)(now out of print)

Wimsatt, W.A. (ed), *Biology of Bats* (Academic Press, New York and London, 1970(vols 1 & 2), 1977 (vol 3))

Further viewing

An audio-visual presentation of forty colour slides with optional tape cassette commentary about the lives of bats in Britain can be obtained from BCT, c/o Conservation Foundation, 1 Kensington Gore, London SW7 2AR.

Information

Bat Conservation Trust (15 Cloisters House, 8 Battersea Park Road, London SW8 4BG. www.bats.org.uk). A membership organisation set up to help conserve bats through education and study. It is a centre for advice and help. Co-ordination of bat groups is carried out by BCT. Members receive the quarterly newsletter, *Bat News,* and junior members receive *The Young Batworker.* A wide range of information leaflets about bat species, feeding and roosting is available, and a list of bat-related merchandise including booklets and slide packs is produced.

The Mammal Society (15 Cloisters House, 8 Battersea Park Road, London SW8 4BG).A national organization seeking to promote interest in the study of mammals. A long-established bat group that helps to co-ordinate and initiate studies on bats amongst its professional and amateur membership. A quarterly newsletter keeps members up to date with recent work. A journal, *Mammal Review,* is also published. A youth section caters for the under 18s.

Fauna and Flora International (Great Eastern House, Tenison Road, Cambridge CB1 2DT). An international organization involved in conservation, particularly of endangered plants and animals. Some of their projects involve bats. FFI produces *Oryx* for its members, which contains occasional bat articles.

County Wildlife Trusts (addresses in local telephone directories or from libraries or via The Wildlife Trusts, The Kiln, Waterside, Mather Road, Newark NG24 1WT). Involved in co-ordinating wildlife conservation at a county level. Many bat groups are closely associated with these trusts.

County bat groups (address from the Bat Conservation Trust). Groups of amateur bat workers involved in bat conservation and research at a local level. These groups are co-ordinated by the Bat Conservation Trust to form a national body of bat workers.

Nature Conservancy Council (Northminster House, Peterborough PE1 1UA). A Government body which promotes nature conservation in Britain. It provides advice on any aspect of bats and the law and it is oblibatory that they be approached if any action that will disturb the bats is envisaged. They will advise on the timing of such actions, methods that must be used and even if the action should be carried out at all. NCC also issue licences to enable bat workers to operate. NCC produce an excellent, informative booklet, *Focus on Bats*, which outlines the law about conservation of bats in Britain.

In the early 1990s NCC split into three to deal independently with Wales (Countryside Council for Wales, Plas Penrhos, Ffordd Penrhos, Bangor, Gwynedd LL57 2LQ), Scotland (Scottish Natural Heritage, 12 Hope Terrace, Edinburgh EH9 2AS) and England (English Nature, Northminster House, Peterborough PE1 1UA).

Institute of Terrestrial Ecology (Monks Wood, Abbots Ripton, Huntingdon PE17 2LS). Operates the Biological Records Centre and publishes distribution maps of bats.

Index